The Story of the FRANK RUSH FAMILY
in the Wichita Mountains and CRATERVILLE PARK

By
Frank Rush III

An Imprint of
Wild Horse Media Group
Fort Worth, Texas

Copyright © 2024
By Frank Rush III
Published By NorTex Press
An Imprint of Wild Horse Media Group
P.O. Box 331779
Fort Worth, Texas 76163
1-817-344-7036
www.WildHorseMedia.com
ALL RIGHTS RESERVED
1 2 3 4 5 6 7 8 9
ISBN-13: 978-1-68179-378-8

ALL RIGHTS RESERVED. No part of this book may be reproduced in any form without written permission from the publisher, except for brief passages included in a review appearing in a newspaper or magazine.

Front cover: A brochure cover from Craterville Park.

To order a copy of
Wichita Mountain Fun

Contact
Frank Rush III
214-725-6727
frankrush3@gmail.com
or
Wild Horse Media
817-344-7036
www.WildHorseMedia.com

This book is dedicated to:
May Rush and Frank Smithwick Rush
Genelle Rush and Edwin Frank Rush
Vickie Foster Rush
Tori West Rush • David Frank Rush
Jodi Rush Cuccurullo • Frank Cuccurullo
Whitney Rush Strong • Taylor Ann Cuccurullo

Special thanks to my beautiful wife Vickie
for her love, devotion, and support.

Contents

Prologue 1
1. The Who Who Magazine 3
2. Frank Smithwick Rush 5
3. Edwin Frank Rush 8
4. Turning Back the Clock 12
5. Emotions 16
6. Wichita National Forest 18
7. Get'er Done Cowboy 22
8. Homecoming 24
9. Ahead of His Time 32
10. Lots of Work to Do 33
11. A Near Miss 46
12. Trees, Trees, Trees 47
13. Mt. Scott 53
14. Treasures 54
15. Places and Friends 57
16. Craterville Park 65
17. Horsing Around 82
18. Jimbo, the Giant Steer 86
19. Indian Curio Store and Museum 89
20. A Turning Point 94
21. Loss and Recovery 95
22. The Midway 97
23. Trains, Trains, Trains 101
24. The Old Swimming Hole 111
25. It's Showtime 115
26. Amazing Acts 130
27. Indian Pow Wows 143
28. Craterville Park Rodeos 153
29. The Rodeo Showdown 165
30. Drawing a Crowd 167
31. Around the World 168
32. National Geographic 172
33. It's the Law 173
34. Special Events 176
35. The Rocking R Ranch 187
36. The Cow in the Well 189
37. Pretty Horses 191
38. Papa Jack Howenstine 193
39. The Land Grab 195
40. New Craterville Park 200
41. Rocking R Ranch Rodeos 221
42. The Big Match 227
43. The New Rocking R Ranch 232
44. Hoofs and Horns 238
45. A Hollywood Visit 245
46. The Meers Store 250
47. Odds and Ends 252
48. Frank Rush Productions 255
49. Commanche County CSI 260
50. Rough Times 263
51. Gone But Not for Good 265

Acknowledgements

Harlow's Weekly, Oklahoma City, OK
Who's Who of America Magazine
New York Zoological Society Bulletin
Blackburn News, Blackburn, OK
Evening Post, Wichita KS
Gateway to Oklahoma History
Lawton Constitution, Lawton, OK
Pawnee Bill Ranch and Museum
Panhandle-Plains Historical Museum
Great Plains Museum
Daily Oklahoman, Oklahoma City, OK
The Review, Apache, OK
Cement Field News, Cement OK
Paul and Jerry McClung
Wichita Mountain Wildlife Refuge
Oklahoma Historical Society
Oklahoma History Center
American Bison Society
New York Times, New York, NY
Special appreciation to Red Steagall and *Somewhere West of Wall Street*
Special appreciation to Nan Taylor Kent editor of *Lawton Then and Now* on Facebook.
Special appreciation to Joey Goodman, Lawton, OK

Most of the news stories, documents, and original photos are saved in the Frank Rush family collection. Some show the year of publication, often in handwriting, and some show no date and/or source. When available, information has been credited to the source. I offer my appreciation to those unknown sources, writers, publications, and photographers.

PROLOGUE

The Frank Rush family lived in and around the Wichita Mountains from 1901 until 1966. During those sixty-five years, it is safe to say, almost every person that lived in southwest Oklahoma visited a site that was managed and/or owned by Frank S. Rush or E. Frank Rush.

This book includes the history of Frank S. Rush, Forest Supervisor of the Wichita National Forest and Game Preserve and founder of Craterville Park. His son, E. Frank Rush inherited Craterville Park and eventually relocated it to the "new" Craterville Park site. E. Frank Rush also owned two Rocking R Ranch locations and two rodeo arena sites while living in Oklahoma. To help keep the names of each Craterville Park less confusing, I will refer to the original location, three miles north of Cache, Oklahoma, and near the south gate of the Wichita Mountains Wildlife Refuge, simply as Craterville Park. I will refer to the second location, north of Altus, Oklahoma, near Quartz Mountain State Park, as the new Craterville Park. The original Rocking R Ranch was adjacent to the original Craterville Park. In 1957 the Rocking R Ranch was moved north of the refuge near Meers, Oklahoma. One rodeo arena location was on the property of Craterville Park and later moved to Cache, Oklahoma.

Our names have been a bit confusing. My granddad, dad, and I have shared the name of Frank Rush. To a high degree, we have been in business together, lived at the same addresses, and had the same phone numbers and friends. My birth name is Frank Rush III. The exact name of my granddad was Franklin Smithwick Rush, and my dad was Edwin Frank Rush. I will refer to Frank S. Rush (1865-1933) as Granddad, his wife, May Seymore Rush (1878-1964) as Mamo, E. Frank Rush (1915-2005) as Dad, my mom Genelle Walker Rush (1915-2009) as Mom, and myself Frank Rush III (1946-) in the first person.

There may be differences of opinion from other sources concerning some topics I talk about. I report the facts as I recall them with firsthand knowledge and use research and references as my guide. In addition, my grandparents and parents collected and saved a great many printed news stories, photos, and memorabilia. One reason for writing this book is to share those personal keepsakes with the public. I hope you enjoy reading about my family and the people and events in their lives.

If I am incorrect about details it is unintentional, and I'll accept responsibility.

One of Dad's favorite sayings was, "If you tell the truth, you can always remember what you said." That's what I'm a fixin' to do.

I write with a great deal of pride about my parents and grandparents, but I am also personally humbled as their son and grandson.

I love what my friend Red Steagall said about them, "They were ordinary people doing extraordinary things."

1. THE WHO WHO MAGAZINE

Franklin S. Rush (Granddad,) b. Tompkinsville, KY, April 6, 1865, was listed in "Who's Who of America" Vol. 15 1928-1929.

The following excerpt is transcribed from *Harlow's Weekly* news article, an early Oklahoma current events journal, published on November 9, 1929. The article was written by Cora Miley.

"In 1928, WHO'S WHO of America, having found his distinction sufficient to include his name in their list, sent Franklin Smithwick Rush of Cache, Oklahoma, a blank to fill out with the account of his ancestry and achievements.

He promptly threw it (the blank) in the corner of his particular domain of the ranch house among the litter of Indian headdresses, Indian beaded jackets, Indian walking canes and coyote hides that reposed there and went about his business. A few days later, Mrs. Rush trying to straighten the melee into some sort of order, found it.

'What are you going to do about this letter, Frank?' she asked.

'What letter?' he asked in his high piping voice?'

'This letter from the Who-Who people?'

'Give it here. I'm going over to Lawton this evening. I'll ask about it. I kinda reckon it's somebody wants to write us up in a magazine,' he replied, stuffing the letter in his hip pocket as he started across the park in his rolling cowboy gait clinking the spurs on his high-heeled boots energetically.

'Say, Jim,' he said to his friend the news dealer in Lawton some hours later, 'gimme a copy of the Who-Who magazine.'

'What magazine?' Jim asked with a puzzled look.

'The Who-Who magazine,' Frank said, speaking a little louder and a little more positively than he had done the first time.

'Why you old fool - term was one of endearment - they ain't no such magazine.'

'I know durn well there is,' Frank said with heat, 'I got a letter from 'em. Here it is.'

'Lemme see it,' Jim said in the tone of cynic. He read it through and then again, his eyes bulging with amazement.

'Why you crazy old thug, don't you know what this is? It's an invitation to be in a book called *Who's Who in America*. It's a book of famous people who's done big things like Mr. Hoover and Governor Smith. There's many a man would give a million dollars to be in that

3

book. Here, take this pen and fill this blank out and send it to 'em quick before they change their minds about putting you in it.'

They didn't change their minds. He's in there…"

2. FRANKLIN SMITHWICK RUSH

Granddad Rush's history notes include the titles of cowboy, ranch foreman, farmer, naturalist, conservationist, Forest Supervisor (Wichita National Forest and Game Preserve), and owner/operator of Craterville Park. Granddad Rush originated the five-year farm plan for the 4-H Club on a national basis. He was a member of the Cherokee Strip Cow Punchers' Association, the Old Time Fiddlers Association, a Republican, Baptist, Mason, Odd Fellow, and Modern Woodsman. In addition, he was a member of The Old Settlers Sons-Daughters Association of Oklahoma, a member of The League of American Sportsmen, held a lifetime Senate Chamber Pass at the Oklahoma State Capital, and carried a badge as a member of the Oklahoma State Bureau of Criminal Identification and Investigation. He married Effie May Seymore Rush, (Mamo) age 17, on December 24, 1895.

Granddad and his work as Forest Supervisor had a historical and far-reaching effect on the Wichita Mountains and Southwest Oklahoma. His position gained stature with local farmers and ranchers, plains Indian tribes, politicians, and the townspeople of much of Southwest Oklahoma. He befriended people including Comanche Chief Quanah Parker and other tribal leaders. He was a revered and respected individual just when the State of Oklahoma was in its infancy and needed men of such stature.

Granddad and Mamo moved to the refuge headquarters, and he began work in 1906. He was officially appointed to the Department of Agriculture as Forrest Supervisor on August 8, 1907, by President Theodore Roosevelt. His assignment was to develop the fifty-nine-thousand-acre wilderness area for public use and to reintroduce native buffalo to the refuge. His starting salary was a tidy $900 per year.

As forest supervisor, Granddad laid out most of the roads we use today, selected locations for lakes and dams, and began constructing the tall game fence around the perimeter of the refuge land. He went to work immediately preparing for the arrival of the buffalo. Once the refuge was ready, he reestablished the buffalo, and later the elk herds that are still there today. During his tenure at the refuge, he accomplished all this and a great deal more.

There was a township named Craterville near the south gate of the Wichita Forest. He had started buying ranchland that included the lots of Craterville Township before 1919. Eventually, the ranch would total 2,700 acres. Granddad moved Mamo and Dad from Forest

Headquarters to the site in 1922, before retiring from the Forest Service on June 30, 1923.

Early on, many people wanted to camp on the property. Mamo noted, "Some of the land was unusable for stock because there were too many people around." Granddad cleared some ground and built fire pits along Crater Creek to consolidate and control camping. Soon he built a dam across a sparkling stream that the Indians called Big Spring, a.k.a, Crater Creek, and opened the swimming pool. Craterville Park and Dude Ranch officially opened for business in 1923 as other attractions were added. Over the years the title "dude ranch" was dropped as "resort" or "amusement park" more accurately described the enterprise.

Frank Smithwick Rush in a beautiful beaded buckskin shirt and his hallmark cowboy hat. c.1927

May, "Mamo", Rush holding an authentic war bonnet in the office of Craterville Park. c. 1950.

3. EDWIN FRANK RUSH

Granddad Rush and Mamo would, no doubt, list their only child, Edwin Frank Rush (Dad, 1915-2005) as their crowning achievement. It was in the late spring of 1915 when the doctor surprised Mamo with the news that the discomfort she was experiencing was a somewhat advanced pregnancy. Apparently, Mamo was not aware she was going to have her first and only child until she went to the doctor concerned about weight gain and nausea. Granddad was 50 years old, and Mamo was 37 when Dad was born on August 31, 1915. One account of Dad's birth in a Lawton newspaper noted, "Cowboy Frank Rush was seen skipping along a street in downtown Lawton today whooping to the public the joyous news of his son's birth."

Dad was eight years old when Craterville Park and Dude Ranch was established in 1923. Over the next decade, he learned and observed firsthand how the park worked. Granddad died suddenly in 1933 from a brain aneurysm. Mamo, Dad, and his soon-to-be bride, Genelle Walker Rush (Mom), were left to continue the operation of Craterville Park. By that time, the park had become, quite literally, the center of family entertainment in Southwest Oklahoma. At the early age of 17, Dad became the wheelhorse of the business that would be the seed stock of his remaining 72 years of life in the entertainment industry.

Particularly in the West, each man's cowboy hat had a unique and identifiable Western crease. Like Granddad, Dad also figuratively wore many hats during his lifetime. Dad was a rodeo performer, rancher, cattle and horse breeder, cowboy, impresario, innovator, idea man, a Wild West show producer, and at different times, owner of three amusement parks. He was a Methodist, conservative, family man, mentor to many and acquainted with people of all statures. His memberships included the American Hereford Association, the American Quarter Horse Association, a charter member of the Oklahoma Hereford Association, and a charter member of the Appaloosa Horse Club of America. He was also a member of the International Association of Amusement Parks and Attractions. Not many days went by when Dad didn't plan a promotion, dream up an innovation, or cause a commotion.

Dad had one peculiarity that anyone who knew him had to get used to. He kept a well-used handwritten phone book containing hundreds of names and numbers. If your name ever got listed, he might call you any hour of the day or night. Luckily, he had a very recognizable voice because he hardly ever said "hello," he would just start talking. Oh, he might have introduced himself to a new acquaintance, otherwise, in the absence of caller ID, the person on the other end of the conversation would be perplexed trying to identify the caller. To make matters worse, at the end of a conversation, he rarely, if ever, said "goodbye." Occasionally he would offer some pleasantry such as "Come see me," but usually all you heard was "click." I was in his office one day when he ended a conversation with a man and hung up abruptly. I admonished him by asking why he didn't say goodbye. He gave me a surprised smile and said, "Because I'm not through talking to him."

E. Frank and Genelle Rush c.1940

E. Frank and Genelle Rush c.1995

The Rush family left to right standing: Frank Cuccurullo holding Taylor Cuccurullo, Jodi Rush Cuccurullo, Frank Rush III, Vickie Rush, Annesa Self, Tom F Self, Tom Self, Suzy Self, David Frank Rush, Tori Rush. Front Row: Whitney Rush, Genelle Rush, E. Frank Rush, and TJ Self. in 2002.

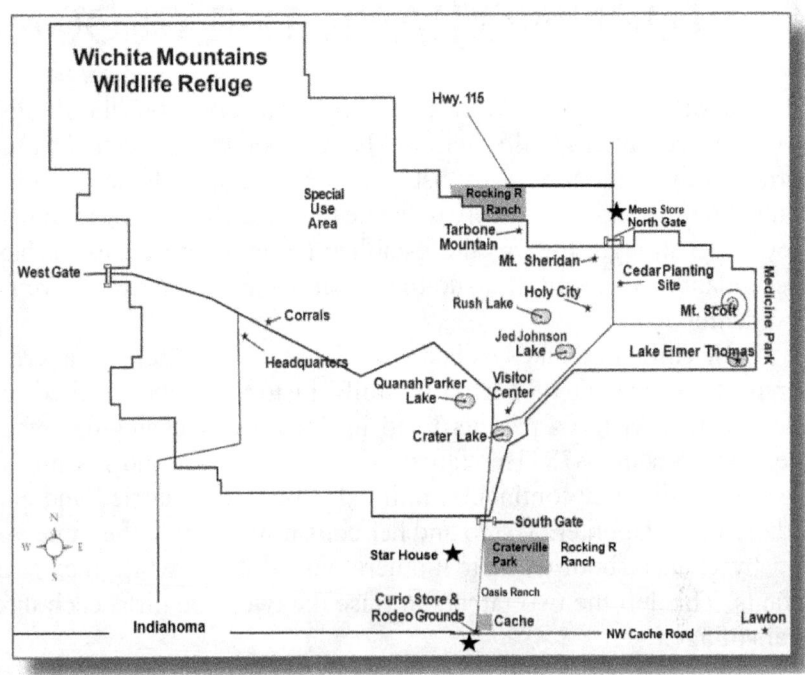

The Wichita Mountains area shows the location of landmarks in the refuge and points of specific interest. New Craterville Park (Not shown on the map). was located 50 miles to the west at the entrance to Quartz Mountain State Park.
This map is not drawn to scale.

4. TURNING BACK THE CLOCK

Granddad Rush passed away before I was born, but the things I have learned about his life help me have a bond that establishes him permanently at the top of my list of heroes. He and Mamo grew into adults literally and figuratively in the heart of the Old West. Obviously, they never thought they would establish an amusement park or have descendants who would pursue that occupation well into the twenty-first century.

Their childhood takes us back to the late 1800s. To put that era in perspective, one bit of Mamo's family history can be recalled and documented. Mamo's parents lived in Spokane, Washington, where she was born in 1878. Her father, Edwin Seymour, and his brother worked on the transcontinental railroad. Both were married and each fathered one daughter. Mamo and her cousin were about the same age, and by chance, both of their mothers passed away while they were infants. This left the two fathers to raise the two little girls, each three years of age.

Edwin Seymore and his brother decided to move back to Coffeyville, Kansas, where they had kinfolks who could look after the little girls. In July of 1880, they traveled east when most people were moving west, and they traveled in a covered wagon. They left Palouse, Washington, on July 27, 1880. My great-grandfather kept a daily journal and related the peril and difficulty of the journey. Imagine two little girls and two men alone in one covered wagon moving across the hot, dusty prairie, through rocky canyons, and crossing rivers without bridges. One passage in the journal tells how they came to a campsite late in the day, only to discover that marauding Indians had vacated it only a few hours before. "The coals of their campfires were still warm to the touch," he noted. Another inscription in the journal, dated August 8, 1880, addresses the plight of Mamo whose mother had passed away only a few weeks before. Edwin wrote, "May says she don't want to ride in this old wagon to see grandma. She has not mentioned your name (her mother) but once or twice until last night after we went to bed. She took to crying for Mama. I thought her little heart would break. She did not like Papa one bit, but after a while she rolled over towards me, put her little arm around my neck, and went to sleep."

Granddad Rush and Mamo lived with their families in and around Cedar Vale and Coffeyville, Kansas, in their youth. Granddad was older than Mamo by 13 years. He made the land run into Indian

Territory on April 22, 1889, when he was twenty-three years old. Mamo often repeated a tail Granddad recalled when riding into "The Territory" in search of his claim. The story is about how he came across a secluded valley with a lean-to hut and a new garden. The Sooners, who lived in the hut, claimed they had just arrived to stake the claim a few hours earlier. Granddad noted onions, boot-top high, in the garden and said to the man, "You better be careful when you plant corn. The seeds could sprout and hit you in the nose as fast as things grow in this valley."

Granddad located and staked his claim near Gotebo, Oklahoma. In 1900, Granddad Rush brought Mamo to live in a sod house he built on his claim. The Wichita Mountains rose just a few miles to the south and were visible on a clear day. I have no record of Granddad visiting the Wichita Mountains at that time, but I'm confident that he must have ventured there often.

A pleasant day at the sod home and homestead of Frank S. "(Granddad)" and May "Mamo" Rush near Gotebo, Oklahoma in 1901.

This interior photo of the Rush home shows Mamo at the upright piano and Granddad holding his fiddle and bow. A neighbor lady was playing her guitar as the onlookers were enjoying the entertainment.

While living there, Granddad studied in the classroom of the great outdoors. He came to understand how the land, along with the plants, and animals that thrived there, could be managed and maintained.

After only a few years, Granddad and Mamo moved to Blackwell, Oklahoma. Granddad was hired by Colonel Zack Miller, one of the owners of the legendary 101 Ranch and the Miller Brothers 101 Wild West Show based in Ponca City, Oklahoma. He later worked for Gordon William Lillie, a.k.a. Pawnee Bill, who owned Pawnee Bill's Wild West Show, based at his Pawnee, Oklahoma ranch. During those times Wild West Shows were more popular than European-style circuses. To my knowledge, Granddad never actually worked in the Wild West shows. Instead, he was engaged as a livestock foreman and ranch manager. But you can be sure, that Granddad's flair for showmanship was influenced by his proximity to those more ornate activities. It even shows in his style of dress and his eventual enterprises in Western entertainment.

His edification grew as he worked on these two ranches. He gained a reputation as an expert in animal husbandry, land management, and wildlife preservation. The moniker "Frank Rush, the Cowboy Naturalist of Oklahoma," was often used about him when written about or quoted.

A naturalist was different yet the same as what we know today as environmentalists. As history shows us, there was little regard for the abundant resources in those days. A prime example was the wanton obliteration of the buffalo. Before 1909 there was no requirement for a hunting license or bag limits on hunting in Indian Territory or Oklahoma after statehood. Granddad was a proponent of game regulation and lobbied territorial appointees and government officials to enact such laws.

The February 14, 1911, publication of The Evening Post stated how he addressed the state senate, "Mr. Rush, Game Warden of the Wichita Mountain Reserve is especially in favor of placing restrictions around the killing of antelope, which stood second to the buffalo in the minds of western plainsmen."

He realized and fostered the concept that settlement and growth of Southwestern Oklahoma could coexist with the bountiful and natural assets the region offered. I believe that Granddad's judgment and visionary ideas, in that regard, are precisely why G.W. Lillie highly recommended Granddad to his friend President Theodore Roosevelt. He was endorsed as the perfect candidate to rehabilitate the buffalo and manage the Wichita National Forrest and Game Preserve.

5. EMOTIONS

By the turn of the century, the buffalo had disappeared from their native home in Oklahoma a few decades earlier. It was not unusual for some of the Longhorn cattle, which the Texas ranchers had grazed in the area on their way to market, to be running feral in the area. Wild horses were still ranging in the Wichita Mountains. The native grama grass, buffalo grass, and mesquite grass provided rich nutrients for the wildlife, however, they were not properly managed or utilized to capacity. Spring-fed supplies of water collected in the granite-lined pools along the creeks. It was an attractive area for various enterprises and pretty much there for the taking.

Cattlemen of the area, including Indians, free-ranged or leased grazing contracts to run their domesticated herds in the mountains. Miners scoured and scarred the flanks of the mountains, especially around Meers and the northern slopes. Around 1900, gold, silver, and copper mines were scattered throughout the mountains, and by some estimates over 5,000 miners poured into the area. Mine tailings, water-filled shafts, and caves are still in evidence in many places today. Rumors of Spanish treasure fueled the gold rush, however, little success was ever realized. Wood was a valuable commodity, and loggers cut timber unabated for mining, bridge, and building construction. Unregulated hunting for sport and sustenance was thinning out or even totally removing many game animals and birds.

Both Indians and some whites resisted the fencing and controlling management of the reservation. And why not? Their unfettered access was taken away. Other people were happy and excited about securing and saving the land from further private development.

In hindsight, we cannot imagine this country without the National Parks, the Forest Service, the state parks, and even city parks that are so precious. However, on a personal note, I must say, there are two sides to that coin. There is a reason that I hold such a profound and fundamental commiseration for the plight of the American Indians and what they lost. Countless volumes recall both sides of their demise and the pioneering of the West. Indeed, this book celebrates how my grandparents helped take the first steps to develop the Wichita National Forest and Game Preserve under government control, and, how Craterville Park was a blessing to millions of people. But make no mistake, Plains Indians were once again on the losing side, otherwise, they would still have what was exclusively theirs, what white men named the Wichita Mountains.

One can also assume that Granddad's friend Quanah Parker, Chief of the Comanches, and other Comanche, Kiowa, and Apache tribesmen must have felt more than a twang of remorse. While progress was inevitable at that point, the whole activity surely cut deep into the hearts of these noble and proud people.

6. WICHITA NATIONAL FOREST

The land we know today is commonly referred to as the Wichita Mountains Wildlife Refuge and had been set aside from Indian territory in 1901 as the Wichita National Forest and Game Preserve under the U. S. Department of Agriculture by President McKinley. It was officially renamed the Wichita Mountains National Wildlife Refuge in 1936.

The area went through a drastic transition during the last half of the nineteenth century. This was a place where only a few decades earlier, literally every human who lived or traveled there did so at their peril. Indian tribes battled each other and certainly became a menace to settlers and soldiers once the natives began to understand the magnitude of the threat the intruders represented. Miners, loggers, traders, and settlers generally eroded the solitude the tribes had, no doubt, taken for granted since before recorded history.

Recognition of the significance and raising broader awareness about the Wichita Mountains is largely credited to President Theodore Roosevelt. Roosevelt had been invited to the Red River Valley for a wolf hunt in the spring of 1905. While hunting and camping along the southern border of Indian Territory, he saw the Wichita Mountains perched on the horizon to the north. Accounts of his wolf hunting expedition tell how his interest grew in the Wichita Mountains natural beauty.

William Hornaday, chief taxidermist at the United States National Museum (later the Smithsonian), had traveled to Montana during the late 1800s to collect and save a few of the last living American buffalo. There is a good bit of history associated with how the captured animals wound up in New York City. Eventually, and with the help of the American Bison Society, the buffalo found a captive home at the New York Zoological Park (now the Bronx Zoo).

By chance, the New York Zoological Park buffalo herd had grown large enough for some animals to be moved to a more natural setting, about the same time as Roosevelt's visit to Indian Territory.

The Wichita National Forest and Game Preserve soon became the site chosen for the relocation by the American Bison Society. This endeavor was the first native animal reestablishment project in United States history.

President Roosevelt, quite literally, had the power and foresight to bring together everything necessary to proceed. One key component was finding a knowledgeable person to do the work. President Roosevelt's friend, G.W. Lillie, a.k.a. Pawnee Bill, recommended Granddad to Roosevelt as the man who could do the job. Roosevelt, Hornaday, Granddad, the Wichita Mountains, and opportunity came together to change the course of history for the buffalo.

In 1906, Granddad accepted the position of Forest Supervisor and moved to the area, even though his official appointment didn't occur until the following year.

President Theodore Roosevelt on the white horse visits with Granddad Rush at the Wichita National Forest and Game Preserve.

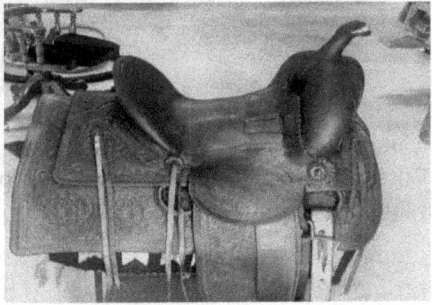

This is the saddle Granddad was riding in the picture with President Roosevelt. It was ordered from Miles City Saddlery, Miles City, Montana, and described as a Premium #2, Powder River tree with "FR carved on the back of the cantle. The cost was $120 including delivery and addressed simply to "Frank Rush, Cache, Oklahoma.

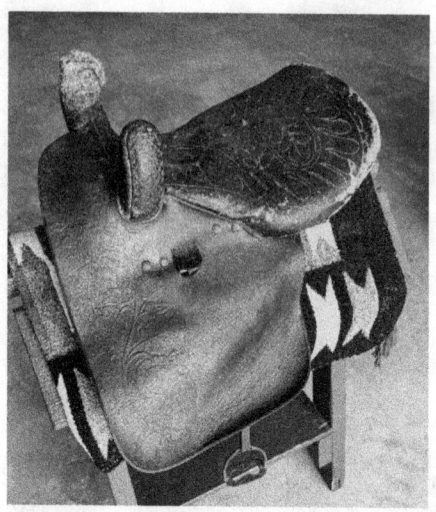

This is my grandmother's well-used and often-ridden side saddle. Men rode "astride," and women rode "aside" in those days. Mamo was known to ride and work as a man might almost every day while living at the refuge.

An early-day scene of the south gate entry to the Wichita Forest and Game Preserve. Notice the small sign, "Hunting and Trapping Strictly Forbidden by Law."

What a challenge and wonderful calling it must have been for Granddad to put together the refuge which would be a protected home for wildlife. At the same time, he would make available and save the primal area for the public to visit and enjoy. Time would prove he was up to the task, and on August 8, 1907, he officially began the job.

Granddad's appointment paper with his official position is shown as "Forest Guard."

7. GET 'ER DONE COWBOY

The Wichita Forest was almost entirely undeveloped when Granddad moved there in 1906. There were few fences or corrals, mostly unimproved roads, and a meager infrastructure. Preparing for the buffalo to return was the goal, and time was of the essence. Statehood for Oklahoma was in the works for the following year, and the return of the buffalo would turn out to be a milestone in the excitement.

The initial buffalo enclosure, fences, and substantial corrals were promptly put in place near headquarters. A local newspaper article reported progress on the fence, "Mr. Rush and Mr. Mantoon (Granddad's predecessor) have surveyed and approved the location for a 90-inch-tall woven wire fence. There are 8,000 acres to be fenced for the buffalo. The government's budget is $15,000, and a contract is being awarded to J. M. Gurley who used local labor for the job."

The fences around the remainder of the Wichita National Forest took years to complete due to the rough and undulating landscape of the area. The boundary surveys of the reserved land paid little attention to terrain, in addition, fencing materials would improve as sturdier steel posts replaced wooden posts.

Granddad Rush was inspecting a section of the early-day fence.

Needless to say, Granddad and his crew had many challenges, but one major hazard loomed ahead of all the others. TICKS! In prior years, Longhorn cattle were driven from Texas to the railheads to the north and brought with them ticks carrying deadly Texas fever. The only preventive to protect the newly reintroduced buffalo, when they arrived, was to eradicate the ticks. Granddad's solution was threefold. First, isolation from other animals was imperative. The second was to burn and reburn the vegetation that harbored ticks in and around the enclosures where the animals would be kept. Finally, creosote oil was possibly the only introduced substance that would smother a tick. Vast amounts of the product were used to soak the soil of the enclosures.

After arrival, each animal would be soaked with the gooey coal tar derivative regularly. Granddad's precautions worked, and the buffalo thrived.

The Plains Indian tribesmen, including Granddad's friend, Comanche Chief Quanah Parker, were elated to see the long-absent buffalo return to the Wichita Mountains. One result of this endeavor was that Frank S. Rush became a revered friend of the Indian tribesmen, and they honored him with their trust, admiration, and gifts of appreciation. It was also a relationship that would pay dividends for both tribesmen and the community surrounding the Wichita Mountains for years to come.

8. HOMECOMING

When the sturdy corrals were built and sufficient pasture had been properly fenced, Granddad asked for the necessary funds and clearance to bring the buffalo home. The infrastructure preparation took place over months, but the actual climax of the event took place over a few days.

After much preparation, Granddad boarded the train in Lawton, Oklahoma, made a brief stop in Washington D. C. to visit the National Museum, then traveled to Grand Central Station in New York City.

While in New York, Granddad oversaw the building of crates that could hold an individual animal with room enough for bedding, feed, and water but portable enough to be loaded onto railroad cars. He meticulously planned for the animals to have no way of escape in transport and was aware that the less they were jostled about, the better for their health and safety. How odd it must have been for him to realize these animals were passing through Fordham Station and the subterranean tunnels of New York City.

The trip back to Oklahoma was filled with scheduling and mechanical issues. The weather was cold and damp, typical of winter in the northeast. Granddad saw to it that the animals were cared for properly, and he also had to coax the railroad agents into special clearances so the railcars could continue to move. Great crowds gathered at train stations in cities along the way, and newspapers reported the progress of the animals.

Granddad Rush at the New York Zoological Park standing on the front of the wagon with a buffalo ready for transportation in 1907.

Frank and Vickie Rush visited the Bronx Zoo Buffalo exhibit in 2016.
This sign is on display at the exact location
Granddad loaded the Buffalo in 1907.

The two train cars that transported the buffalo
displayed signs announcing the unusual cargo.

This photo is of the buffalo enclosure at the New York Zoological Park.

At last, the train pulled onto a siding at the station in Cache, Oklahoma. Indian chiefs, tribesmen, cowboys, town folk, farmers, ranchers, and politicians had gathered for the event in advance. The Indians had bittersweet satisfaction when the crates containing their beloved buffalo were off-loaded onto horse-drawn wagons for the final leg of their journey home. Among the Indians, celebration and ceremony were at a peak. Orations and kudos were on the agenda, but Granddad was eager to bring the buffalo journey to an end. The buffalo were home.

Calves born in the spring of the following year grew fat on the native grass and never realized that their sires and dams had been to The Big Apple. After their return to the West, the herd grew and prospered under Granddad's supervision and husbandry.

An article in the New York Zoological Society Bulletin Vol. XVI No. 57 in May 1913 by Elwin R. Sanborn reported; "Five years have now elapsed since the New York Zoological Society presented fifteen bison to the United States Government and established them as a national herd in the Wichita Forest of Oklahoma. The time elapsed is sufficient to demonstrate either the success or failure of the undertaking. The inception of the plan found many who were willing to wager that at the end of the first year, not one animal would survive the ravages of Texas fever cattle ticks. To those doubting Thomases, it becomes a pleasure to say that the Wichita bison form the most perfect herd of wild hoofed animals this writer has ever seen." The article also stated, "Warden Frank Rush has worked unceasingly to put the surrounding country in touch with the Preserve."

The long journey home ended at Cache, Oklahoma, where the crowd of onlookers gathered for a welcome of the buffalo.

Two workers posed with a buffalo crate at Cache, Oklahoma.

A mule and horse-drawn wagon train traveled the last few miles across the prairies on the way to the holding pens at the Forest Headquarters pasture.

"Black Dog" was billed as the "largest buffalo in the world," weighing 2800 pounds, and the monarch of the herd. This is the image from which James Earle Fraser designed the Buffalo Nickel coin for the United States Treasury according to the Wichita Mountain Wildlife Refuge.

A crowd awaits the buffalo's arrival near Forest Headquarters.

Men were preparing to release a buffalo at the corrals.

Granddad sprayed buffalo with creosote oil to prevent ticks from transmitting Texas fever to the unacclimated buffalo.

Buffalo in the original corrals near Forest Headquarters.

Two unknown uniformed men (left) pose with Frank S. Rush and Mamo Rush for a keepsake photo. c.1908.

Early day "prairie hay" bailing in the Wichita Forest.

9. AHEAD OF HIS TIME

Granddad was a proponent of reintroducing several species to the forest reserve. His innate responsibility to flora and fauna did not start after he arrived in the Wichita Mountains. Prior evidence of this is evident in a 1905 article written by Granddad in the *Blackburn News*, Blackburn, Oklahoma, where he lived at the time. The lengthy article decries the declining fate of indigenous animals, game birds, and even songbirds.

The article reads in part, "To the True Sportsman. In the last ten or fifteen years, there has been a great change in the fauna of North America. The development and perfection of long-range guns and smokeless ammunition leaves the game, both large and small, absolutely in jeopardy. Hunters are more numerous than ever before. All of the large animals are growing smaller (in number). All large animal species in the United States are being crowded into smaller acreages every year and every day." At the end of the article, Granddad admonished all readers, especially sportsmen and zoologists, to "get busy."

His wisdom and concern were undoubtedly influenced by the near annihilation of the American Bison species. Only a few decades earlier, between 1830 and 1885, the animals that were the life providers for the Indigenous population had nearly been wiped from the face of the continent. Once estimated to be forty million in number, the remaining scattered remnants numbered fewer than 600 animals by 1895.

On a personal note, and with the luxury of hindsight, Granddad could not foresee the future of the wildlife issue even by half.

10. LOTS OF WORK TO DO

The Wichita Mountains are among the oldest mountain ranges in the nation. They lay at the western end of a subterranean mountain range that exists to the east and spans several states. Only millions of years of wind and rain erosion could grind away the sharp corners of the majestic rocks to a relatively smooth surface while leaving some precariously balanced atop the sub-structure. The resulting sand, gravel, and stones washed down into the creek beds and valleys and made a handy resource for endemic construction material. Settlers could hitch a strong team of horses to a sturdy wagon and harvest the produce of Father Time's abundant crop of cobblestones. The headquarters buildings were frame and log structures at first. Later more durable cobblestone structures were built. Some of those buildings still stand and are unusual in their appearance.

A picture of Granddad's and Mamo's home at Forest Headquarters. c. 1909

The headquarters building with typical cobblestone construction, and a water fountain in the front yard.

The roads laid atop broad ridges or hogbacks between the valleys and creeks. Granddad designed the natural curve of the roads to take advantage of the scenic vistas as they wound through the area. Low water crossings and bridges were built to accommodate narrow creek crossings along the way. Turnouts for scenic views are great places to observe the animals, foliage, and ancient hills.

The road-building crew working under the direction of Granddad.

Plenty of projects could be planned and completed in short order. Others required completion as time, manpower, and funds allowed. For example, grass management and water availability could be dealt with by rotating the herds between pastures. A reliable water supply was imperative for each pasture. While fresh spring water flowed in some places in most years, it was insufficient, so small dams were constructed to pool the supply. Planning for larger lakes was incorporated into the long-term program for water storage, fishing, waterfowl habitat, and visitors' recreation. Some of Granddad's forethought didn't come to fruition for years. It wasn't until the 1930s that the Civilian Conservation Corps (CCC) and the Workers Progress Administration (WPA) put people back to work during the Depression. Case in point, most of the larger dams constructed by the CCC and WPA were planned by Granddad years earlier. Lake names such as Jed Johnson, Quanah Parker, French, and Elmer Thomas were chosen in honor of worthy individuals. One particularly beautiful lake was named Rush Lake in Granddad's honor.

An early-day aerial photo of Rush Lake.

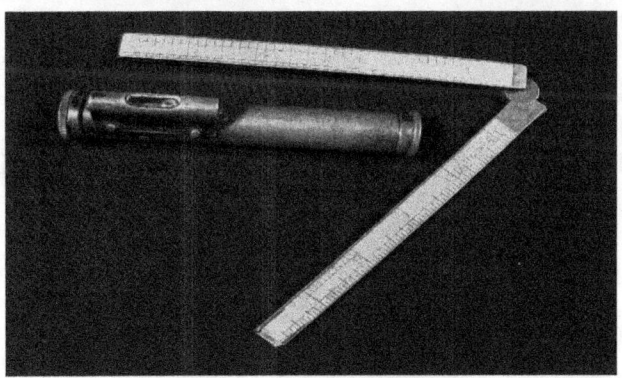

This is Granddad's folding ruler and handheld leveling scope used for projects such as road construction, the location of dams, and his early efforts considering the feasibility of a road up Mount Scott.

In 1910, while living at Refuge Headquarters, Mamo was primarily responsible for reestablishing wild turkeys once native to the area. The turkey population had been depleted. Only a single turkey was reported near headquarters in 1909. Mamo raised chickens for eggs and meat. I remember Mamo telling me she asked Granddad to locate some breeding turkeys. He acquired two hens and a tom. Mamo made use of the chicken pens behind her house at Forest Headquarters, and the turkeys produced twenty-three hatchlings that season. She released the birds a year later, and they did not stray far from headquarters. In 1912 the United States Biological Survey shipped 13 wild turkeys to the Wichita Mountains from Atoka, Oklahoma. She kept those birds captured until they became acclimated before releasing them. The genetics in the offspring of those birds still populate the refuge and southwest Oklahoma today.

Mamo's contribution is scarcely mentioned in the shadow of Granddad's efforts to repopulate the buffalo, elk, and other species. She was not paid or praised for her accomplishment in reestablishing the turkey population, however, it was a significant project.

Mamo was known to be a hard worker at Forest Headquarters. She rode horseback alongside Granddad daily as he went about the affairs of management. As was the custom of the day, she is always pictured wearing a riding dress and riding a ladylike sidesaddle while horseback.

She was hired as a clerk in the Forest Service by the U. S. Department of Agriculture in 1910. As you can see from her employment document, her salary was $2.00, not to exceed $300.00 in any one year. Granddad's starting salary in 1907 was $900.00 per year. In 1909, he was hired for additional duties as a Game Warden of the Forest Service for $1200 per annum. He earned a promotion and raise of $1400.00 per year as Forest Supervisor in 1910. All totaled, they were doing pretty well because the purchasing power of their combined annual salary of $2,900 would amount to an estimated $95,000 in 2024.

United States
Department of Agriculture,

Washington, D. C., February 18, 1910.

Mrs. MAY RUSH - - - - - - - - - - - - - - - - - -, of the State of OKLAHOMA -, is hereby appointed A CLERK,

In the Forest Service,

in the United States Department of Agriculture, at a salary at the rate of TWO ($2.00) - Dollars when actually employed, per diem, on the miscellaneous roll paid from the fund appropriated for "General Expenses, Forest Service;" or from any other lump fund appropriated for the Forest Service to which the salary is properly chargeable. Total compensation not to exceed $300.00 in any one year.

The above-named appointee is hereby required to take the Oath of Office immediately and file the same, together with a statement of legal and actual residence and personal record, with the Appointment Clerk in the Department of Agriculture, and report of duty in writing, to the District Forester, Albuquerque, N. M., and in person to the Supervisor of the Wichita National Forest, Cache, Oklahoma, (District No. 3) - - - - - - - - - and be subject to the rules and orders of the Secretary of Agriculture. This appointment shall take effect on February 18, 1910.

Acting Secretary of Agriculture.

Mamo's paper approving her position as a Forest Service clerk.

A family outing for Mamo, Dad, and Granddad. c.1920

A gathering at Forest Headquarters with the recognizable fountain in the foreground. The person on the far left is Frank Bohan-Forest Ranger, Mamo is second from left, and Granddad is far right. The others are unidentified.

In 1910, Granddad arranged for a herd of eleven pronghorn antelope to be shipped from Yellowstone Park. Unfortunately, he did not travel to Idaho to foster the animal's well-being, as he did with the buffalo and elk. Sadly, some died in transit, and the balance developed an unknown internal disorder after arriving in the Wichita Mountains. Within three years, they suffered the same fate. The effort to reestablish pronghorn antelope in the Wichita Forest failed to succeed.

A rare picture of antelope in the corrals north of Forest Headquarters. c. 1911.

There was another endeavor that never came to pass. Granddad made a concerted effort to establish a herd of Karakul sheep in the reserve. Exactly why is a mystery to me. Charles Goodnight, the famous owner of the JA Ranch in the Palo Duro Canyon, near Clarendon, Texas, communicated in several letters with Granddad about obtaining some Karakul breeding stock. The wool from this exotic breed was a favorite of Navajo Indians for rug weaving.

Shown here is a typed and hand-signed letter from Charles Goodnight about leads for obtaining Karakul sheep. Judging by Goodnight's signature, a new-fangled typewriter made the letter more legible. Apparently "white-out" wasn't available yet.

39

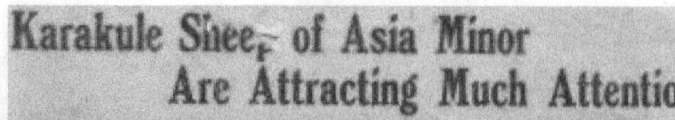

This is an advertisement for the Karakul sheep that Charles Goodnight sent to Granddad.

A February 14, 1911, newspaper article in *The Evening Post*, Wichita, Kansas stated, "In addition to about 75 native white-tailed deer, there are now twenty-three buffalo and seven antelope on the reserve, all in excellent condition. The reserve now has but one bull elk." The native elk had been hunted to extinction in the area during the 1880s, so there was certainly a need to rekindle their presence.

In the shadow of Granddad's endeavors with the buffalo, is his important accomplishment of reintroducing elk to the refuge. Granddad's epic trip to bring the buffalo home from the New York Zoo laid the foundation for his trip to St. Anthony, Idaho in 1912. At the railhead there, he received a small herd of elk donated from the newly established National Elk Refuge near Yellowstone.

On March 14, 1912, a local news article from an unknown source announced in part, "RUSH AND ELK ARRIVE. Three weeks ago, Frank Rush, Game Warden in Charge of the Wichita National Forest, left here for St. Anthony, Idaho to return with a fine heard of elk consigned to the Wichita Forest. On March 8th, he returned to Cache with eight head crated and expressed (by train). There are more to follow. Mr. Rush expected to return with seventeen head, but various reports give just seven more to arrive by later express making fifteen head. Besides this consignment of elk, one large elk bull from Wichita, Kansas has been here over a year and (he has) become well acclimated. Mr. Rush will keep them in pens for two or three months before releasing them in the 8,000-acre buffalo pasture. He desires everyone to come see while there is an opportunity."

Elk from Idaho being reintroduced and held in the corrals near Forest Headquarters. c.1912.

Elk and buffalo shared corrals near Forest Headquarters. c.1913.

The elk, like the buffalo, thrived and the herd eventually grew to a number that allowed thinning. After the elk population reached sustainable numbers, the government ordered elk from the Wichita

Forest to be reintroduced to the Pisgah National Forest near Asheville, North Carolina. Granddad's expertise in crating and shipping animals was once again put to beneficial use. It was necessary to dehorn the bull elk captured for shipment. The cow elk, of course, escaped that humiliation. Granddad had suitable crates constructed, oversaw the loading of the animals onto train cars, and accompanied the unusual cargo to their new home in North Carolina.

This picture was taken at the Pisgah National Forest in Asheville, North Carolina showing Granddad delivering crated elk to a forest ranger and a forest supervisor. The crates Granddad had built were remarkably similar to the Buffalo crates from 1907. Again, the antlers were sawed from the bull elk for aid in transportation.

The New York Times recounts the delivery of the elk to Pisgah National Forest and Game Preserve. The caption explains how the elk were brought from the Wichita Game Preserve in Oklahoma. Frank Rush can be seen in the foreground on horseback.

Granddad unintentionally and unofficially started the longhorn herd in 1910 with a single specimen named Old Whitey. The story goes that Granddad had seen Old Whitey leading a herd of cattle being driven to market a few miles west of headquarters near Mountain Park, Oklahoma. By that time, most cattle were more domesticated beef cattle, not typical longhorns, so Old Whitey stood out because of his color and impressive horns. Old Whitey was a "bell steer" and had the classic look of the longhorn breed. He purchased Old Whitey for $11 and kept him as a pet at headquarters.

Before Granddad's retirement in 1923, a group of qualified people had begun selecting prime specimens of Texas Longhorn cattle from a wide-ranging area throughout Texas and the Southwest. In July of 1927, the Forest Service finally allocated $3,000 to purchase 27 longhorn breeding animals and three steers as the original foundation stock for the Wichita Forest. Granddad, though retired, assisted in the project by offering experience and advice, however, most of the work was done by Forest Ranger Earl Drummond.

Old Whitey at Forest Headquarters.

Granddad's collection of various skulls and horns from the herds that ranged near Forest Headquarters.

Once the herds of buffalo, elk, and Longhorn cattle grew to such large numbers that they had to be thinned out. Especially in the early years, the annual Buffalo roundup in the Wichita Mountains was always a wild affair. It seemed there was seldom a roundup in which some daring cowboy or their horse wasn't injured. Over time, corrals were built with solid fences and walkways on top so the animals could be handled safely.

Large crowds of buyers and interested locals attended the event which garnered national attention. The buffalo were culled and auctioned off only for their meat. No live animals were sold. Later, the policy changed, and the buffalo were sold at auction or donated for breeding stock allowing the creation of many private herds. In 2020 the buffalo auctions were discontinued and the WMWR joined the National Wildlife Refuge System in providing a 100% donation of all surplus animals to Indian tribes and intertribal organizations.

The annual Texas Longhorn sale was also held for decades, making it possible for breeders and enthusiasts to purchase animals. As a result, the genetics of nearly all the privately owned buffalo and most of the animals registered in the Texas Longhorn Breeders Association of America can be traced back to the foundation herds in the Wichita Mountains. The elk numbers are kept in check largely by an annual lottery for hunting permits.

In the early days, only old buffalo cows and young bulls were culled and sold at auction. The animals were slaughtered on-site for human consumption. While the animals were perfectly fit to eat, they could not be sold live because buffalo can carry a hard-to-detect disease called Bangs or Bovine Brucellosis. This malady resulted in requiring the animals to be slaughtered at the refuge corrals so the meat could be consumed. If the animals were sold live, the disease could decimate domestic herds.

From my experience, I can verify that school districts, including Cache ISD where I attended school, bought the meat, and served it in the cafeteria. The meat was generally from old, tough, grass-fed animals and not nearly as tasty as grain-fed, lean, and healthy buffalo meat available today.

Heck Schrader and Elmer Parker, long-time refuge employees and genuine cowboys, were riding hard to pen buffalo for culling in 1948.

11. A NEAR MISS

There is a long-forgotten and short-lived controversy that fortunately did not come to pass. Just before Granddad's retirement, in the spring of 1923, rumors spread from Washington D.C. about the forest being closed to the public and used solely for game preservation. The news came as a surprise to everyone involved in southwest Oklahoma, including Granddad.

A newspaper story on April 29, 1923, reported a letter from District Forester F.W. Reed to 6th District Congressman Elmer Thomas assuring him, "The Wichita National Forest will be open to the public at all times." Reed emphatically denied that the Forest Service supported any movement to close the Wichita Forest. Further, there would be improvements made to attract even more tourists.

Public access to the refuge has been and will remain a blessing we take for granted. While there were government agencies and proponents of closing the refuge, we can all be thankful the idea was short-lived.

Granddad was already establishing Craterville Park and Dude Ranch near the front doorstep of the forest and counting on tourists to be a large component of his venture. Luckily the issue was squelched in short order, and I'll bet he gave a huge sigh of relief.

12. TREES, TREES, TREES

Early settlers in the area had taken their toll on the old-growth trees by harvesting them for mining, fuel, and building construction. Granddad understood that the reforestation of native cedar trees and other species in the area was much needed. He planned a nursery where seedlings would be planted, tended, and transplanted as they matured. A site, near the north gate of the refuge, was chosen in 1912. It was a field with rich soil, and an ample water supply was nearby. They planted thousands of seedlings spaced about thirty inches apart.

Over time, many small trees were transplanted as intended. However, many were cut at ground level and used as building material. Some of the remaining stumps can still be seen today. By removing every other tree, this "thinning" process allowed room for the ever-growing trees to spread into the newly vacated space. After over a century, the remaining trees appear somewhat stunted and thin growing due to the cramped quarters, yet compelling in their entirety.

The original name of this project was known by the refuge staff and locals as the "Cedar Planting Site." Other descriptive names, including the parallel forest or the haunted forest, are newer adopted titles. There has been a good bit of confusion and misinformation about who planted the seedlings and when this nursery was established. Some have misreported the project was a CCC or WPA endeavor in the late 1930s. There are also stories saying ghostly voices can be heard when no one is near. I have doubts about the unworldly fantasies, but they do add to the public fascination of the site. I also doubt that my grandparents ever envisioned what the lasting mystique of the Cedar Planting Site holds today. This remains a popular stop where tourists observe the trees in surreal alignments that stretch to every point of the compass.

The trees have been threatened by forest fires numerous times. I was a witness on one occasion which occurred on the blistering hot and windy day of August 4, 1963. A range fire started when artillery practice 5 miles to the south and on the Fort Sill firing range ignited the grass. The wildfire, backed by the gale-force wind, raced quickly north over the low hills and jumped the highway between the Holy City and the entrance to Mount Scott (Hwy 49). Several other ranchers and I, with water tanks and pumps mounted on our trucks, soon gathered on the highway between the foot of Mount Sheridan and the Ceder Planting Site. A couple of trucks from the refuge showed up, and there was little doubt the Cedar Planting Site and the forest between us and the foot of Mount Scott would soon be in ashes. At an astonishing speed, the conflagration swept north and onto rancher Wayne Rowe's pastures. In the distance, we could see and hear random cedar trees explode in balls of flames. At that juncture, we 30 or so firefighters were no match for what happened. The fire burned for two days consuming a few sections of prime private ranchland and hundreds of acres of forest in the refuge before being controlled. Surrounded on all sides, the Cedar Planting Site trees stood defiant. I believe the trees were spared in tribute to Granddad and Mamo, but more likely by the Grace of God.

The army did send troops and a bulldozer to help contain the 1963 fire. By the second day, the fire was still not close to containment. Concern mounted the fire might jump Hwy 115 and head west up and beyond Mount Sheridan. It is difficult to visualize, nevertheless, a brave army soldier drove a bulldozer and scaled the northeast flank of Mt. Sheridan to the rock escarpment crowning the mountain. The firebreak, cut by the dozer on the steep slope, did indeed stop the fire, at least at that location. The scar left by the bulldozer was visible for many years until vegetation reclaimed the trail.

If anything about the fire was amusing, it had to be the ranch cowboys watching the young army recruits extinguish a smoldering buffalo chip. Try as they might, once on fire, a buffalo patty can smoke for days even after being dunked in water, slapped at with a wet feed sack, or even stomped to pieces. The valuable but seldom-needed lesson is if you ever fight a grass fire in a buffalo pasture leave the chips to smolder.

The Cedar planting site in 1912.
Granddad is shown holding a shovel second from the left.

The Cedar planting site near the foot of Mt. Sheridan.
Granddad is kneeling second from the right.

Frank Rush III on a visit to the Cedar Planting Site
February 2024, just 112 years later.

Granddad Rush is on the left with friends posing by a gnarled cedar tree trunk. This oddity was collected in the nearby hills and displayed at Forest Headquarters where it was a popular photo subject for many years.

In June of 2024, Vickie and I visited the beautiful city of Asheville, North Carolina. While there, I stopped by the office of the National Forest Service. I noticed a showcase in the lobby containing early-day Forest Service equipment, memorabilia, and a single photograph. By coincidence, it is the same photograph of which I have an original from Granddad's collection. It was a surreal experience to find Granddad pictured while attending the first Southern Forestry Conference held in Asheville, July 11th through the 15th, 1916. The group convened at the Battery Park Hotel and visited the Biltmore Estate. Speakers at the conference were an impressive group of professors, scholars, and nationally known forestry experts.

By chance, immediately following the conference on the evening of July 15th, two hurricanes collided over western North Carolina dropping 22 inches of rain in 24 hours. The resulting flood caused 80 deaths including some of the Biltmore Estate employees. Apparently, Granddad was on the train back to Oklahoma, narrowly missing the historic flood.

Later that year, on October 17th, 1916, Pisgah National Forest was officially established, and on November 7th, 1916, President Woodrow Wilson proclaimed Pisgah a National Game Preserve.

Granddad (seated, fifth from left) attended the first Southern Forestry Conference in Asheville, North Carolina in July 1916. He also attended similar events in El Paso, Texas, and Alamogordo, New Mexico.

Dad's earliest public accomplishment ranges back to his boyhood days when he came up with the idea of planting a tree on the state capitol grounds in Oklahoma City. Dad had read the poem "Trees" by Joyce Kilmer, who had died at Flanders in World War I. He asked Granddad if he could plant a tree in honor of the war hero. A newspaper story relates the event.

E. Frank Rush (Dad), with a shovel planting a tree in honor of Joyce Kilmer on the grounds of the Oklahoma State Capitol in 1925.
Also pictured are a troop of Boy Scouts, Martin E. Trapp, Governor of Oklahoma (center), and Frank S. Rush (Granddad) wearing his always recognizable cowboy hat.

A picture and headlines from the 1925 news story about the tree planting on the state capitol grounds.

A letter addressed to Frank Rush Jr. (Dad) Craterville, Oklahoma, from a lady who attended the tree planting ceremony states in part: "I much enjoyed your kind courtesy in the memory of Joyce Kilmer today. I am copying a couplet from a friend of mine for you… 'Trees are both human and divine. They are the handshake of God with man."

13. MOUNT SCOTT

Mount Scott is the most famous landmark of the Wichita Mountains. At 2,464 feet in elevation, the view from the top is awe-inspiring.

Granddad was instrumental in the early and ambitious concept of building a road to the summit. Granddad and Mamo traveled to Colorado, to see firsthand, the Pikes Peak Auto Highway soon after it was completed in 1916. He realized that a similar road spiraling to the crest of Mount Scott might be possible and returned home enthused with the idea. Armed with nothing more than determination, a hand-held surveyor's scope, and some geologic survey maps, he marked the general path on which the road would eventually be built.

There is a good deal of documentation about Mount Scott Road because it was an on-again-off-again project for years. Once the project finally got underway in the 1930s it incurred trouble including the bankruptcy of a contractor and labor issues. During and after completion, washouts, rockslides, and erosion plagued the work. The result is a narrow two-lane highway largely completed by CCC and WPA workers. The road and crown jewel of the Wichita Mountains was dedicated and opened on August 16, 1938.

The construction workers surely realized the road would be enjoyed by many tourists. They may not have fully contemplated how romantic, inspiring, and productive a moonlight drive to the top of Mount Scott with your favorite girl might be.

This is a beautiful and unusual aerial view of Mount Scott looking west from the Medicine Park area courtesy of GW Aerial Photography.

14.   TREASURES

Granddad held a fair number of personal memberships and interests, as mentioned in his earlier introduction. He proudly served as President of the PTA in Cache and President of the Cherokee Strip Cow-Punchers Association. His favorite pastime was playing the fiddle, and he won occasional championships. He served as President of the Old Time Fiddlers Association.

Granddad was especially interested in a new organization, the 4-H Club. He is credited as being the originator of the 5-year farm plan for 4-H boys and girls on a national basis. He also created the Frank Rush Award going to a 4-H Club boy or girl for the best-written 5-year farm working plan. The Award was presented annually at the Oklahoma Livestock Show in Oklahoma City starting in 1927.

Frank S. Rush and Olin Butler of Guthrie, Oklahoma, the 1926 Frank Rush Trophy winner.

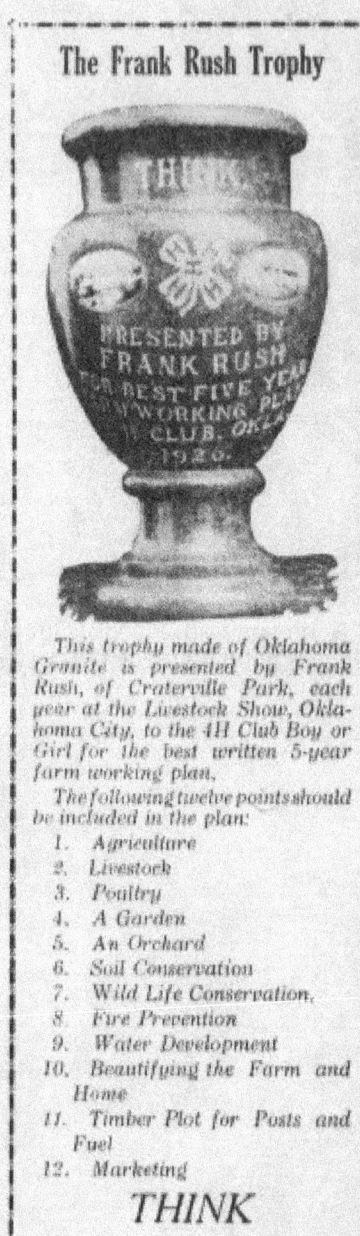

The Frank Rush Trophy award description and outline for the 4H Club best written 5-year working plan. c. 1926

15. PLACES AND FRIENDS

Granddad and Mamo traveled a decent amount while he was the Forest Supervisor. I assume those excursions were pleasurable, but they always included something Granddad might want to explore concerning the Forest Reserve. They visited Pike's Peak as mentioned earlier. They visited the Black Hills National Forest of South Dakota in 1918, well before Mt. Rushmore was started. They visited New York City, the Statue of Liberty, Charles Goodnight's famous JA Ranch in the Texas panhandle, and G.W. Lillie a.k.a. Pawnee Bill at his ranch in Pawnee, Oklahoma.

Charles and Mary Ann Goodnight owned a historic ranch in and around the Palo Duro Canyon in the heart of the Texas panhandle. It is likely, that the only remaining specimens of the Great Southern Buffalo herd, at that time, had survived slaughter in the canyon on the Goodnight ranch.

Charles Goodnight

Granddad and Goodnight had become acquainted because of Granddad's involvement with the buffalo re-establishment in the Wichita Mountains. On October 6th and 7th, 1916, Charles Goodnight produced a silent movie staged on the JA ranch depicting a buffalo hunt in the canyon. An Amarillo newspaper headline referred to the event as "The Plains Last Buffalo Hunt." Granddad, Mamo, and Dad (Dad was one year of age) were invited to witness the making of a silent movie recounting Indians killing a buffalo. Granddad had arranged for a group of Kiowa Indians, including his friend Horse from southwest Oklahoma, to reenact the buffalo hunt for the movie. Horse was the man chosen from the Indian group to actually kill a single animal with his bow and arrow. Thousands of people attended, and the following day Granddad, Mamo, and Dad were honored guests at a picnic where the slain buffalo was served as the main course. This historic film can be viewed on the Portals of Texas History website.

The trip from the forest headquarters to the ranch near Clarendon, Texas was not a speedy 125-mile journey, but Granddad and Charles had plenty to talk about when they were together. The buffalo were, no doubt, a frequent subject, as well as the profound history of the JA ranch, the Palo Duro Canyon, and the Goodnight/Loving Trail.

My grandparents continued their long-lasting friendship with his former boss and friend G.W. Lillie and his wife Mae. Remember Lillie had recommended Granddad to President Roosevelt for Granddad's Forest Service job. Like my grandparents' friendship with other people, they visited each other's homes on occasion. Recalling G.W.'s history, he was best known as a showman and owner of the highly acclaimed Pawnee Bill Wild West Show based in Pawnee, Oklahoma. He also became more interested in the preservation of buffalo as a species during the years he and Granddad were acquainted. As with many of Granddad's friends, I would love to have heard their conversations.

G.W. Lillie, "Pawnee Bill"

Coincidently, Dad, who was six years old, and Lillie's son, Billy Lillie, had played together at their Pawnee, Oklahoma ranch only a week before Billy's tragic death. Billy accidentally hung himself while climbing on a radio tower the following week. Soon after Billy's death, Dad received a handwritten note from Mae Lillie expressing her love and sorrow for Billy, and imploring Dad to "be careful and not climb too high."

Chief Quanah Parker lived in his historic Star House on West Cache Creek from 1889 until he died in 1911. The Star House was a gift paid for by Texas rancher Burk Burnett in partial consideration for leasing tribal land in an area known as the Big Pasture in Indian Territory.

Quanah's fabled home and ranch of a few thousand acres bordered the south fence of the Forest Reserve and lay a couple of miles directly west of where Craterville Park would later be established.

Once the chief realized the old ways of the plains Indian tribes were little more than history, he acclimated very well to the "white man's path." Quanah and Granddad became close friends from the earliest moments Granddad arrived at headquarters in 1906. No doubt, Granddad's involvement with the return of the buffalo was responsible for Quanah's regard for him. Quanah looked to Granddad for advice on business dealings and tribal issues, and Granddad's rapport and contact with government officials and politicians were certainly beneficial to the tribes.

There are interesting stories about why Quanah had large white stars on the roof of his house. My favorite version is a report that when Quanah had visited a military base, perhaps back east, he had seen stars on the roof of the general's quarters. He said he wanted bigger stars painted on his house but was told only generals were afforded such an honor. He replied, "I'm a general. I get stars."

Quanah had imposed his philosophy on other interesting occasions. For example, he was told that it was not the way for white men to have more than one wife, so he should tell his five wives that four of them must go. Quanah was certainly not keen on that idea, so he responded, "You tell 'em."

There is a long background story on how Quanah's Star House got where it is and its poor condition. I know the story well because in 1956 I was 9 years old and accompanied Dad to visit the Star House a few times. Dad often visited with Neda Birdsong, the daughter of Quanah, and Topay, Quanah's last living wife. As far as I know, they were the last inhabitants of the house before the 1957 Fort Sill "Land Grab." (The Land Grab is the subject of Chapter 39.)

During the battle to keep the Corps of Engineers from condemning the Star House, Quanah's ranch, Craterville Park, and other land, Dad would pay a visit to Topay and Mrs. Birdsong to help them understand what was about to happen. They would sit on the east side of that fabled house enjoying the shade and cool evening breeze and visit, often until dark.

Meanwhile, I had the run of the yard and porches. On occasion, I would go inside the screen door to see a long dinner table where, unbeknownst to me at that time, a host of famous people had dined. Guest included President Roosevelt, Will Rogers, and famous Texas cattlemen Charles Goodnight, Dan Waggoner, and Burk Burnett, among others. Military Generals and Indian chiefs such as Comanche chiefs Wild Horse and Powhay, Souix Chief American Horse, and even the venerable Geronimo enjoyed their repast at that table. I did not, at that time, realize Granddad and Mamo were also invitees to the Star House on occasion.

One of those visits is still crystal clear in my memory. On that particular occasion, I had ventured inside the house when Dad called me out to the porch and told me, "Mrs. Birdsong said you can play inside but don't go upstairs." Well, I went back inside with a sudden and irresistible urge to satisfy my newly aroused childhood curiosity. Giving them a couple of moments to continue their visit, I snuck up the broad staircase, quietly opened one of the big doors, and peeked inside. There, piled high and overfilling the entire room was a cache of Indian artifacts the inventory of which I could not begin to count, but no doubt the trappings and memorabilia of the old chief himself. Amazed, and honestly a little spooked, I quickly but quietly made my way back down the stairs and hurried back outside. I never told Dad what I did and saw, and it's not important, except that I didn't obey him. But to this day, I would bet the inventory of that room could fill an interesting museum, and I could easily be one of the few white people to bear brief witness to the site.

Without question, the ladies realized that the approaching and bitter condemnation of their ancestral home was just another chapter in the storied history of the forced changes of the Comanche by the government.

Although her birthday is unrecorded, Topay was about 90 years old at that time. She spoke enough English to communicate and was obviously distraught about what was fixing to happen. She was a hauntingly beautiful but old woman, with skin that looked like fine but wrinkled and bronzed lamb skin. Her hair was mostly gray and held back by beaded Eagle bone hair clips. She was a mythical work of art to me, but I do not believe she had one tooth in her head. I remember well my curiosity when she would smile or laugh, as she frequently did, and I wondered how she could chew her food.

In owing to her depleted dental situation, Dad usually took her fresh oranges, those being her favorite. He would peel and section an orange for Topay, which she gummed with delight and leaving a few stray drops of juice on her somewhat whiskered chin.

Quanah and Granddad were close friends until Quanah passed away in 1911, thus Topay was well acquainted with Granddad. I also know she was a fond friend of Dad at Craterville Park. Topay and almost all the Parker family members attended the powwows at Craterville Park.

This is the point in my story where it becomes part true and part speculative.

The true part: As reported in a story in the Lawton Constitution on July 25, 2000, written by Paul McClung, Quanah was buried at Post Oak Cemetery when he died in 1911. The McClung story reports in part, "It was not the first time Topay had seen what greed can do. In 1915, vandals disinterred her husband and robbed his grave of valuables. An account of the day said one of Parker's wives came to mourn over the grave one Sunday morning and fainted when she saw the partially filled grave with bits of the casket and bones lying here and there. The bones were washed, dried with costly blankets, and reburied in a new casket. In later years Topay personally made large bouquets of paper flowers to place on the grave."

As the Land Grab came to fruition, Craterville Park was being moved. Mrs. Birdsong and the other landowners had been given a date by which they must vacate. Quanah's body was to be moved from Post Oak Mission to Fort Sill the following year in 1957.

As usual, the conversation between Dad, Mrs. Birdsong, and Topay was not compulsory for my young ears. But at one point, Topay stepped inside and returned to the porch with a small brown box. She was carefully showing Dad the contents, and I could see her eyes tear up. They talked for a few moments in hushed voices, and that whole scene sure made me want to peek. I moved closer as she held the box a little lower so I could see. Inside were some worn and broken strings of colored beads, a few buttons, a half-dollar-sized tarnished medallion of some sort, and parts of two tortoiseshell hair combs with bits of hair tangled in the combs. Without explanation, she closed the box and pressed her crooked old finger to her lips in a silent gesture of secrecy. Heading down a dusty section line on the way home I asked Dad about the box. I don't remember his exact words, however, he did say something to the effect it was from an old Indian grave.

The speculative part: Over the years I have given that moment a good deal of thought. I have absolutely no proof or way to confirm anything in this regard. I offer my thoughts only as a hypothetical fantasy. That being said, given the timing, the bitterness, and the visceral unrest Quanah's approaching exhumation surely brought on the living Comanches, and the spirit of Quanah, I wonder if those trinkets were from Quanah's grave.

More to the point, I've had a lifetime friendship with lots of Indians, and I have a deep regard for their nature and how they view things from their unique perspective. Besides, if those trinkets and possibly his remains were secreted away, it seems to me like something someone might have done to achieve one last victory for Quanah Parker.

The Indian woman, Topay, was the wife of the great Chief of the Comanche. Mrs. Birdsong was a first-generation descendant and his blood flowed through her veins and his spirit was captured in her soul. Their trusted white friend, my dad, gave them his time and good counsel, but at some point, they said one last goodbye. I was just an obscure witness, but recalling those visits is fulfilling to me.

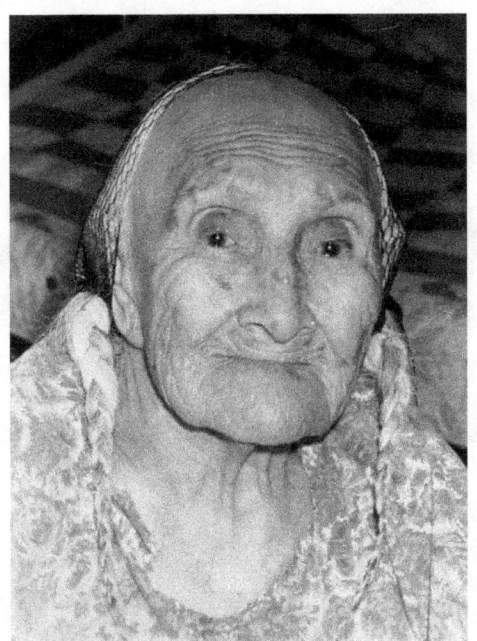

Topay, the last living wife of Quanah Parker.

The dining room in the Star House was where so many people visited Quanah Parker.

An early-day family picture of Quanah's Star House.

Shortly after Granddad's friend, Chief Quanah Parker, passed away on February 23, 1911, Granddad served as pallbearer at his funeral. Granddad is shown with his black cowboy hat in his left hand and holding the casket handle with his right hand.

16. CRATERVILLE PARK

I regret not asking more questions about how, when, and in what order buildings and attractions were added and actions took place. I find myself writing a book about my family's business a century ago and admittedly there are some unanswered questions. However, the juxtaposition and exact order of events seem to me to be less important than the occurrences and park attractions themselves.

The township, known as Craterville, was born as a result of mining activity in the area. Of course, Indians had inhabited the Wichita Mountains for untold centuries. The Craterville Township had been developed by optimistic investors hoping to turn a profit, and indeed, a few people purchased lots for cottages. A handful of cobblestone or wood frame cabins were built on those lots, however, most of the lots were never sold to individuals much less developed. Even after Granddad was open for business, he bought the last few lots as they became available.

There is no way of knowing when the idea of a park first sparked in Granddad's mind. He started planning his move, buying the land, and even establishing his home a few years before retirement. Once he retired, Craterville "the Park" happened in a rush. (No pun intended.)

Craterville Park (1923-1956) was fifteen miles west of Lawton and three miles north of Cache. It is a beautiful country surrounded by granite mountains. Many people, including our family friend, Mrs. Jerry McClung of Lawton, remembered Craterville Park as "A Magical Place." It was often advertised as the "The Family Playground of Southwest Oklahoma." Indeed, the location was stunning and majestic. To anyone who loves the many vistas of the Wichita Mountain range, the Craterville Park site would be among their favorites.

Like many other families Mom's parents, Dilmus Walker, a.k.a Dandy, and Maudie Walker, and their three kids, including Mom's sister Jessie and brother Royce Dan, visited Craterville Park on summer vacations to camp and play. Dad and Mom met at the park's skating rink on one of those outings. Romance ensued and they became engaged in March of 1933 and married two days after Dad's eighteenth birthday on September 2, 1933.

During their engagement, tragedy suddenly struck the family. Just one day after Granddad's sixty-eighth birthday, on April 7, 1933, he died suddenly of a brain aneurism. Granddad's sudden demise was a shock to his family. His death left Dad, Mom, and Mamo to continue his dream of operating the park. Without those three people and their willingness and ability to accept responsibility in his absence, many lives in Southwest Oklahoma would have been altered. Most assuredly, the balance of this book would contain many blank pages. Thankfully, the things Granddad initiated continued almost seamlessly, especially under Dad's stewardship.

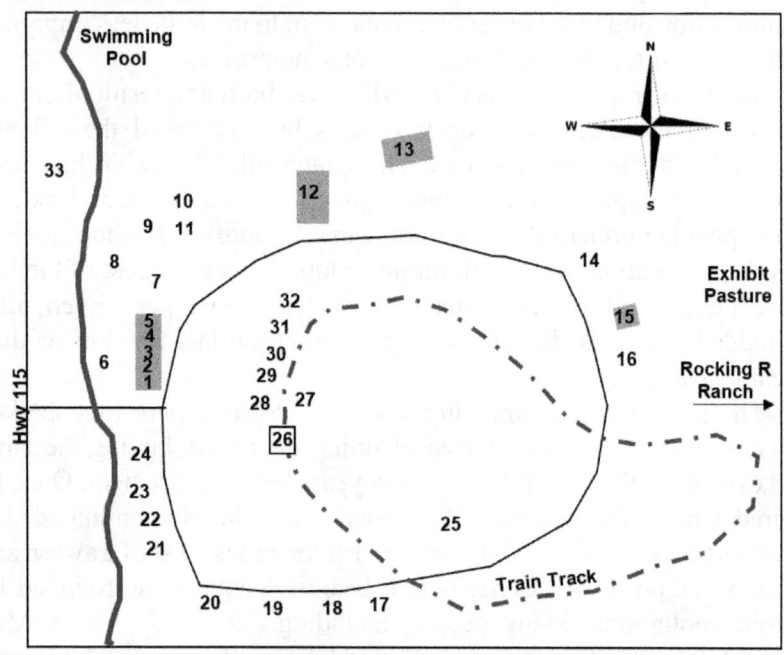

Craterville Park attraction locations. c.1957
*Shaded rectangles are buildings still standing in 2024.
This map is not drawn to scale.

1. Grocery Store*
2. Park Office*
3. Glass House*
4. Dark House*
5. Pretzel Ride
6. Campgrounds
7. Refreshments
8. Mini Golf Course
9. Skating Rink
10. Bumper Cars
11. Arcade
12. The Rush Inn
13. Shop Building*
14. Mamo's House
15. Rush Family Residence*
16. Employees House
17. 80 Days Water Tower
18. Monkey Zoo
19. Shetland Pony Ride
20. Saddle Horses
21. Horse Barn
22. Jimbo Exhibit
23. Rattlesnake Pit
24. Indian Curio
25. Show Stage
26. Train Ride Station
27. Fly-O-Plane
28. Roto Whip Ride
29. Bulgy Fish Ride
30. Midge-O Racer
31. Carousel
32. Rock-O-Plane
33. Boy Scout Building

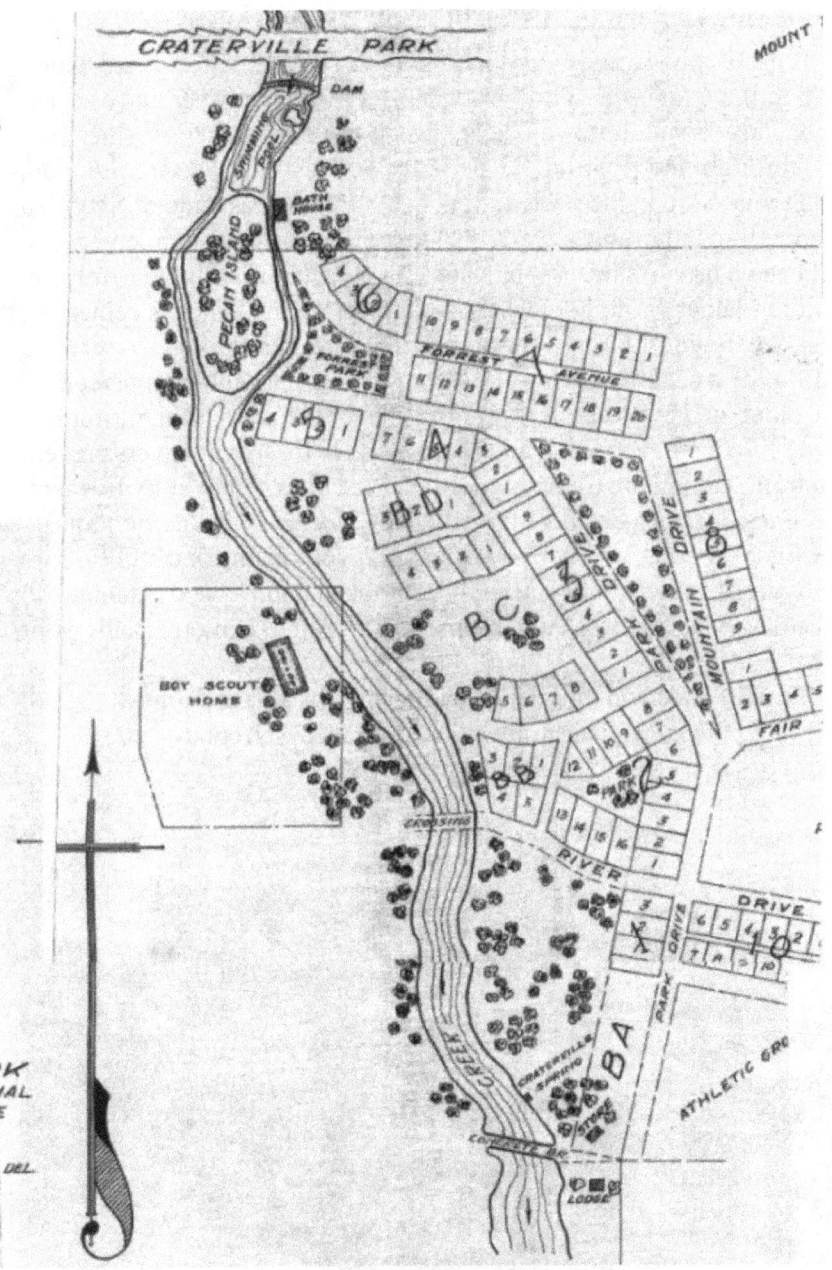

Platted on Jan 23, 1902, this is a hand-drawn plot of Craterville Township. The heart of Craterville Park would later be located approximately where the words athletic grounds appear in the lower right corner. This map is not drawn to scale.

Visit the park property for your personal experience.

It is relatively easy for historians or people who would enjoy visiting the Craterville Park property. As of this writing, daily access is generally available seven days a week. Post visitors must enter Fort Sill through the Bentley Gate at 6796 Sheridan Road, Lawton, Oklahoma. Stop at the post visitors center on the east side of Sheridan Road before entering the staffed checkpoint. At the visitor center, you will need a driver's license, or state ID for each person in your vehicle. Children under 17 do not require a pass. Inside the visitor's center is a kiosk where you fill out a short questionnaire, submit your paperwork and ID for a security review, and obtain your pass for each person 17 and older in your vehicle. Camp Eagle is the army's name for the Craterville Park site. Ask if any restrictions or troop maneuvers prevent you from visiting the Camp Eagle area. Plan to exit the fort by five p.m. A *Natural Resources Sportsman Servies Map* is available on request. Ask for directions or better yet, Google on your phone or car GPS from 6796 Sheridan Road to Camp Eagle. It takes about twenty minutes to drive the route. Allow as much time as you can to explore. Enjoy your visit!

To save time and you may also register for a pass online at:
https://pass.aie.army.mil/steps/branch_selection

A scenic view photographed for a postcard shows Craterville Park. The park appears to be packed to capacity.

When Dad took the reins, at seventeen years of age, tourists and campers frequented the park in even larger numbers, and more attractions were added. On the land Granddad had purchased for pasture, located to the east of the center of the amusement park, Dad introduced purebred horses and cattle and titled the operation the Rocking R Ranch.

The frequent rodeos and Indian powwows Granddad established were expanded in scope. Both events were staged in the Exhibit Pasture. Free shows and concerts increased in popularity on the show stage closer to the midway. Special events and camps were introduced. The reputation of the park as a clean, safe, and affordable destination was the subject of many conversations and newspaper stories. Few people were living in the area that did not visit Craterville Park.

An early day view from atop a nearby mountain and looking northwest. This photo was taken before the addition of many attractions.

Craterville Park artistic advertising poster.

While Craterville Park and Dude Ranch occupied the ground from 1923 through 1957, camping out on summer vacations was in vogue. Storytelling, sing-a-longs, handheld fans, kerosene lanterns, tents, and camp fires were utilized, rather than televisions, refrigerated air conditioning, portable generators, RVs, and gas-fired barbecue grills. The simple pleasure of being out-of-doors, and away from home and work held the same appeal for many families then as now.

Granddad recognized people would not only come to camp but if recreation was available, a profitable enterprise could blossom among the granite hills. The park's pristine beauty and the amusements' locations combined, made it a perfect site for Craterville Park. The following description and some old photos fall short of the experience, but let's journey to that magical place as best we can.

To begin our journey, traffic turned east off Highway 115 three miles north of Cache. (This is not an access point today). The road rolled over a couple of low hills, through the oak trees, and crossed the Crater Creek bridge. The road made a big circle taking in a large flat expanse where most of the attractions were located.

The original Craterville Park entrance sign on Highway 115 and a bevy of beauties!

View of the road to Craterville Park from Highway 115 in 2024. (This is not an access point today).

An aerial photograph of the early day midway, the show stage to the left, and the Indian curio store in the upper right corner. c.1930s.

Turning left, the main building housed a grocery store, the park office, and originally the park museum. As of this writing the building still stands, and the rock facings have withstood the decades beautifully.

Early on, the original museum was relocated from the north end of the building, then new attractions were installed including a glass house maze and a dark house maze. Both the glass and dark mazes were rooms filled with walk-through obstacles. The glass house was simply full-length glass panels and was confusing even though customers could see in all directions. The dark house was similar, but customers had to feel along plywood panels in complete darkness. The dark house was scary, fun, and probably a little too personal at times as customers groped their way along.

An early-day view of the main building housing the grocery store, park office, and Playland, judging from the cars probably from the late 1930s

An early-day aerial view of the main building with the name changed to Funhouse on the far-right end. Judging the cars this time, maybe in the early 1950s.

The main building looked much the same at about 100 years of age when Vickie and I visited the Craterville Park location in February 2024.

The grocery store sold fresh meats and fruit, eggs, milk, vegetables, and canned goods along with a supply of camping gear, swimsuits, cooking utensils, and first-aid needs. There were shelves filled with comic books and magazines, candy jars, bottled soft drinks, and a freezer box filled with containers of ice cream from Fairmont Dairy in Lawton. The store offered about any item campers might need. Picture postcards printed in color were popular at three for a dime. In addition, it only cost two cents for a postage stamp, plus there was an official US Post Office where mail could be cancel-stamped, "Craterville Park, Oklahoma." Upstairs, rooms were provided for employees to live in while working at the park.

In 1950 an extension was made to the north end of the building for a Pretzel ride. The Pretzel ride was a serpentine dark ride and was one of the last attractions added at Craterville Park. At the loading area riders were seated in cars powered by an electrically charged track leading through doors designed to keep out the light as they entered a very dark room. Once inside, about a dozen "tricks" or animated spooky figures would suddenly light up when a passing Pretzel car would trigger a switch. Jumping, screaming, and holding each other close would inevitably result. The Pretzel was a big hit with dating couples looking for a few moments of "alone time."

Dad, employee Happy Hull, and an unidentified cowboy pose for a newspaper photo with a Pretzel Ride car. c. 1950

Just north of the main building was an icehouse which was considered a luxury for campers simply because there was no portable refrigeration. The icehouse also provided an ice supply for the park's refreshment stands and restaurant.

Along Crater Creek just behind the main building were campgrounds. Huge cottonwood and pecan trees shaded the area and dozens of persimmon trees lined the creek. A low water crossing allowed campers to cross Crater Creek to access additional camping space.

An 18-hole miniature golf course built of concrete and cobblestone was north of the camping area. The fairways were hard-packed with gravel, but the putting surface consisted of ground walnut or pecan hulls. When the surface became bumpy, the required maintenance included releveling the hulls, wetting, and tamping with a heavy steel plate. In the absence of synthetic carpet, the fairways and "greens" were remarkedly smooth and durable. The natural slope of the land and the cobblestone stone obstacles on the fairways were added features. There was a fee to play including a club and ball.

The unique cobblestone miniature golf course was a popular attraction for players of all ages. c. 1940s

Vickie and I visited the Craterville Park site in February of 2024 and found most of the miniature golf course still visible in the underbrush.

This is a cobblestone tunnel or obstacle located on the miniature golf fairway. This picture was taken in February 2024, proving the durability of good workmanship and cobblestones.

To the southwest of the miniature golf course, a spring-fed creek ran along the west side of the developed part of the park. The most used name was Crater Creek, even though I've seen it referenced by other names. It was also the same stream that kept the swimming pool, just upstream, full of fresh water.

To the east of the golf course and back on higher ground was the skating rink building. The huge frame structure, built in 1926, had a high-grade hardwood skate floor and large screened openings that could be closed in winter. Clamp-on skates with leather buckles were attached to your shoe soles, and away you went for a fun one-hour skating session. "A million dollars' worth of fun, for only 25¢/hour," was painted on a posted sign. The music played on the nickel jukebox, and the first thirty minutes were for clockwise skating only. A fifteen-minute session of reverse skating (counterclockwise) let everyone unwind and kept all the "lefties" from complaining. You got to skate clockwise again for ten minutes. The last five minutes were for speed skating only, and you were warned to get off the floor if you didn't feel brave. If you wanted to skate for another hour you had to buy another ticket, or Shorty Rowe, the rink supervisor, would call your name and send you to Mamo at the ticket booth.

Youth groups often visited the park by the truckload to go skating. This photo was taken before the "Skooter Cars" addition on the east side of the structure.

Inside view of a good crowd on the hardwood skate floor.

A 2024 reference photo showing the area where the skating rink once stood.

The electric bumper car building joined the skating rink, and there was a nickel arcade where you could try a pinball game, or get your fortune told by a Genie in a glass box. Another machine could mash a penny into a bracelet charm with Craterville Park embossed onto one side of the reshaped copper.

Mamo sold skating tickets in a glass-framed, elevated booth, and woe be the poor soul who misbehaved under her watchful eye.

Occasionally, she would collect a silver dollar from a customer. Silver dollars were common in those days, and they made a perfect gift for me when I helped her sell skating tickets or do her chores. She told me I was working, but what she was teaching me was how to make change and be courteous to customers. I still have a few of those silver dollars along with precious memories of my grandmother and the skating rink.

Continuing around the perimeter of the park, The Rush Inn, a seasonal restaurant, welcomed guests, employees, and families where delicious meals were prepared by cook Jimmy Stone. I recall Alma Kirk running the food line and making sure every child who passed along in front of her had washed "both hands" before eating. Fresh homemade ice cream was offered to all who "cleaned their plate."

Upstairs over the restaurant was the employees' dormitory. Only the cook and single men were allowed to room there.

The Rush Inn. The tall tower was a Hi-striker machine. The building on the right is the Merry-Go-Round.

The Rush Inn cafeteria line. The young man seated in the striped shirt is Frank Rush III. (I got to eat with the big boys!)

The Rush Inn interior with varnished knotty pine tables, bentwood chairs, and a mounted buffalo decoration keeping watch.

The Rush Inn is still standing in 2024.

Granddad and Mamo's house originally stood where the Indian Curio Store replaced it. In 1934, after Granddad died and Mom and Dad married, two homes were built on the east side of the complex. They were Mamo's house and our family's home next door. Eventually, a third house was built for Bob and Alma Kirk when they came to work at the park.

17. HORSING AROUND

Further around the circular road to the south was the monkey zoo, the saddle horse rental stable, the Shetland pony stable, and the main horse barn where trail rides were organized.

Horseback riding was a natural fit for Craterville Park and renting saddle horses was a huge drawing card from the beginning. Originally, the horse corrals were smack dab in the middle of the action, and for years riders were free to ride anywhere they chose. There were inevitable problems caused by horse manure on the midway and safety with horses mixing with cars and foot traffic.

In the 1930s saddle horse riders had the run of the property including the midway area.

To solve the problem a new Saddle Horse building was erected on the south end of the park grounds in 1949. A fenced riding lane along the base of the mountain led to the Exhibition Pasture allowing the riders more space. More room and shade were provided in the building where "dudes" could select a mount and get riding instructions before a real Western riding experience. The open and scenic space of the Exhibition Pasture was the perfect place to enjoy riding at will. A park employee kept watch, mostly to keep riders from running the horses and overestimating their acquaintance with riding skills.

A Shetland Pony stable was also built so parents could lead a pony with their child in the saddle. On busy days, as many as 40 or 50 riding horses and a dozen or so Shetland ponies would be saddled. To find so many gentle, sound, and attractive horses was always a challenge.

A view looking south from the main building shows the monkey zoo on the left, the new Saddle Horse building, and the original Indian Curio store sign on the right. c. 1952.

The new Saddle Horse barn and Shetland pony corral. Part of the monkey cage is visible, far left, and the round steel ticket booth would be a collector's piece today.

Trail rides into the foothills of the Wichita Mountains were a favorite attraction at the park.

On the southwest corner of the complex was the Live Rattlesnake Pit. The rattlesnake pit was a popular attraction where, for a small fee, you could look down on a desert setting with writhing clusters of live diamondback rattlers. Girls always screamed when the snake keeper tickled their ankles with a string on a stick, and every viewer was glad the snakes were in confinement rather than roaming the hills around the park from where many were captured.

SNAKES ALIVE! There're 180 of them in this recently-built pit at Craterville park. All are deadly diamond-back rattlers with exception of two cottonmouths and three or four coachwhips. Manager Frank Rush purchased the reptiles at Waynoka this week. The snakes will become a regular part of Craterville's exhibits. They will be cared for by snake handler J. C. Henderson. (Staff Photo)

If you're squeamish about snakes, this Lawton Constitution news story is not for you.

Yet another exhibit at the park was the monkey cage. It was a chain link enclosure about 35 feet square and 20 feet tall. There were usually 12 to 15 Rhesus monkeys, and their disposition was perfect for display. They also had a deserved reputation as thieves. Even though a six-foot-tall security fence surrounded the enclosure which kept the monkeys and onlookers a couple of feet apart, they could still swipe anything you had in your shirt pocket, eyeglasses and cigarettes being their favorite. Anytime the park was open the monkey cage drew a crowd.

18. JIMBO, THE GIANT STEER

Located between the rattlesnake pit and the Indian Curio Store, was possibly the most remembered attraction at the park. His name was Jimbo," The World's Largest Steer"! A special building for Jimbo was erected in 1954, late in the history of Craterville Park. From the day the exhibit opened, almost every person who entered the park gladly paid a quarter to get a look and everyone got their money's worth.

Dad had been acquainted with R. L. Davis of Scottsdale, Arizona, who owned a huge mixed-breed steer, Cimarron, which he displayed at state fairs around the nation. Cimarron resembled a water buffalo but was billed as the only animal alive being a buffalo/Brahman cross. Cimarron's advertised weight was three thousand, one hundred and forty pounds. Dad had tried to buy Cimarron, but Mr. Davis wouldn't sell the animal. Dad soon contemplated searching for his own "world's largest bovine."

By chance, in 1954, the owner of the stockyards in Lawton called Dad and told him to hurry down because he had something to show him. Dad picked me up after school in Cache, and when we pulled up to the sale barn there was a giant brindle steer of mixed breeding looking over the top rail of a six-foot fence. The animal had been the family pet of a farmer, Mr. Tomkins, in Duval, Oklahoma. We were told that the farmer's children bottle-fed the orphaned calf, and he was so gentle that they just kept feeding him and letting him grow into a giant until he was too big to handle. Dad didn't want to seem too excited, but he knew the animal was bigger than anything he had seen and would make a great attraction for the park.

Jimbo was not only big for a three-year-old, but he continued to grow after Dad purchased him. He kept him on display for many years at Craterville Park, then at new Craterville Park, and later at the Indian Curio store in Cache. At two bits a look, the animal paid for himself many times over.

In 1964, Jimbo became ill and started to lose weight. My brother-in-law Tom Self and I loaded him in a trailer and drove to the Paul Jones Lumber Yard scales in Cache. We weighed the truck and trailer with Jimbo inside. We then took Jimbo to the Kelsey Veterinary Clinic near Porter Hill, Oklahoma. Doctor Charles Kelsey decided intestinal surgery was the only slim chance the animal had of recovery. He also told Dad that the surgery would probably be fatal. It was a tough decision, but Dad gave the okay. Jimbo did not survive, but Doctor Kelsey found the cause of his demise. Many bovine animals ingest small pieces of metal in their feed, which becomes embedded in the stomach lining and intestine. The result is known as Hardware Disease. Most animals are slaughtered long before this becomes a life-threatening problem. Jimbo succumbed to a handful of short pieces of wire and other small metal items he had consumed in his hay and feed over the years.

Only after Jimbo had gone on to greener pastures did we fully realize how big he was. Tom and I returned to Mister Jones' lumberyard the same afternoon and weighed the truck and trailer minus Jimbo. The net difference in weight was 3,425 pounds. We estimated, conservatively, that Jimbo had lost another five hundred pounds during his three-month illness, so his total weight was at least 3,900 pounds.

Frank Rush admires his favorite animal of all time. This picture is the "real deal." Jimbo really was this big.

Frank Rush III petting Jimbo.

Dad called Mister Davis in Arizona and told him we had lost Jimbo, and we knew for sure that Jimbo weighed about 3,900 pounds before he became ill and died. Mister Davis revealed that Cimarron was never heavier than 3,200 pounds, but to maintain some bragging rights, he reminded Dad Jimbo was a muley (no horns) and Cimarron had large horns.

Mr. Davis's photo of Cimarron was a present to Dad shortly after they became acquainted.

19. INDIAN CURIO STORE AND MUSEUM

Completing the tour around the loop was the Indian Curio Store and Museum building.

By far, the Indian Curio Store and Museum housed the most history about Craterville Park. The variety of merchandise was expansive. Beautiful beadwork from the local Comanche, Kiowa, and Apache tribes was offered for sale. Granddad and Dad purchased lesser amounts of locally made items, simply because the local tribes did not make a cottage industry of their handy work as was the case with tribes out west.

Traders representing trading posts in Arizona and New Mexico visited the park in the off-season presenting their wares and taking orders. Authentic Chimayo and Navajo Indian rugs and blankets were colorfully displayed. Clay pottery of several varieties, woven reed baskets, and especially turquoise and silver jewelry were among the best sellers. The quality of most items available would be considered high-end and collector items today. For one reason, the artistry was authentic. The most skilled artists, at that time, had just started to add hallmarks to their work and the better-known masters demanded a premium price. Also, the good "old pawn" pieces generally contained a better grade of silver and especially a higher grade of turquoise. Over time, stabilized or treated turquoise has mostly replaced the high-grade turquoise from the famous mines of the West. In some cases, orders were placed for late winter delivery, but in many cases, Mom and Dad simply selected the purchases for the store directly from the salesman's display. I must admit Mom would occasionally purchase a piece of jewelry for her use, some of which I still have.

Minnetonka moccasins from Minnesota were good sellers. While the shoes were not Indian-made, the style was popular and the name and the packaging went well with the store's other offerings.

For many years award-winning Frankoma Pottery had the best reputation and name recognition of any dinnerware in the West, especially Oklahoma. Dad and Mom were acquainted with the company's owner John Frank of Sapulpa, Oklahoma, and literally ordered truckloads of pottery to sell in the store. Recalling the space in the store displaying Frankoma Pottery, I am sure it was the top revenue producer.

Most of the Indian-made replications were purchased from the Pawnee Bill Trading Post in Pawnee, Oklahoma. There are other references in this book recounting my Granddad's acquaintance with Pawnee Bill. During the time Dad owned Craterville Park and later, new Craterville Park and the Indian Curio Store at Cache, he was probably Pawnee Bill Trading Post's best customer. Replica tom-toms, tomahawks, gourd rattles, arrowheads, miniature tepees, headdresses, trinkets, and curios of wide descriptions were all "Hand Made by Real Indians" and ordered and sold in great quantity.

The original Indian Curio Store

The Interior of the original Indian Curio Store.

Another interior view of the original Indian Curio Store.

A section of the store housed a museum and exhibit of memorabilia Granddad Rush had collected over the years. The displays included notable articles from his accomplishments, documents of historical significance, Indian artwork, beadwork, and costumes he had received from the Plains Indian tribes. He had lobbied for Indian rights and welfare on their behalf with his contacts in the state and federal governments. He welcomed them to Craterville Park and organized the Indian Fair, in return, the tribal leaders took any opportunity to bestow on him their finest objects of Indian artistry. Many of these articles were on display.

An extensive collection of arrowheads, spear points, and scraping knives was displayed, all of which had been collected by Granddad in the Forest Reserve and in and around the Craterville Park property.

Frank Rush and Frank Rush III in front of the Craterville Park Covenant inside the Curio Store Museum shortly before it burned in 1955.

The building also housed the original buckskin copy of the Craterville Park Covenant establishing an agricultural Indian fair. This artifact alone was worthy of attention because of its artistry, it was the cornerstone document establishing the official Indian Fair at Craterville Park and later the American Indian Exposition in Anadarko, Oklahoma. (The Craterville Covenant will be covered in Chapter 28.)

Granddad Rush standing in front of the original Craterville Park Covenant in 1924.

20. A TURNING POINT

In 1933, after Granddad suffered a brain aneurysm, he was taken to Southwestern Hospital in Lawton where he survived for three days. He was awake and aware, and had the presence of mind to tell Dad, "Genelle is going to be the only partner you'll ever need."

He passed with his family at his bedside, while outside on the lawn of the hospital many of his Indian and white friends quietly held a vigil.

A Lawton newspaper headline read: STATE INDIANS LAUD LIFE OF WHITE FRIEND. The subtitle stated, "Tribal Leaders Point to Colorful Figure as Their Brother. On Sunday, April 9, Frank Rush, southwestern Oklahoma's most famed pioneer, was buried in the granite-clad Wichita Mountains. The grave site is near the front of Highland Cemetery on Sheridan Road in Lawton. Over 1,000 Indian and white friends were in attendance and Indian speakers, in their native tongue, eulogized Rush as their leader, advisor, director, and best friend. The big First Christian Church was filled to capacity with hundreds standing outside in an overflow crowd. It is probably the county's largest funeral."

Southwest Oklahoma had lost a leader, the Indian tribe members lost a friend who championed their causes, but Mamo and Dad had lost the most. To their credit, they did not falter. A business had to be tended to and challenges lay in store.

One unforeseen issue soon surfaced. If you have ever heard the term "Indian giver," it is derived from a long-standing custom by many tribes. If a gift was given to you, it was yours as long as you were alive. When you went on to the spirit world, the custodianship of the article was no longer yours, and the gift giver could retrieve the gift. The custom was widely accepted as proper etiquette among Indians, but in later times, the term itself became a slur to describe a greedy or stingy person.

Soon after Granddad died, many Indians came to Mamo and Dad to reclaim gifts given to Granddad. The issue quickly got out of hand because multiple individuals claimed ownership of some particular article in the collection. Indian friends of Mamo and Dad advised them to refuse all requests because hard feelings and disputes would cause more harm than good. Dad recalled how he and Mamo would tell inquiring Indians that the items were also given to her, and she was still alive, and besides most of the items were on display in the museum. To their credit, the Indians understood, and few, if any, held a grudge.

21. LOSS AND RECOVERY

The museum continued to grow after Granddad's Death. Dad was no stranger to collecting and continued to add items of interest to the assemblage. Fortunately, the museum displays had overflowed, and many items were displayed or stored in other buildings.

Had it not been for an unfortunate accident that collection would fill a large display in museums today.

Mom and Dad were away visiting friends in Fort Worth in the late winter of 1955. Annie Duggins was the store manager and had left the building one evening after receiving a large shipment of goods for the upcoming season. An electrical fire started around 5 a.m. and spread quickly throughout the building. By the time Bob Kirk, the park foreman, was made aware of the blaze, there was no time to save the building or the contents. Bob lamented later that if he had just had the presence of mind to back a truck into the sidewall of the building and collapse the section that housed Granddad's collection, he might have saved some of the keepsakes. Dad and Mom returned home, and I recall how completely shaken Dad was. He seldom cried, and I know his heart was broken. This was one of only two occasions in my life that I saw Dad sobbing. To his credit, he hugged Annie and Bob and said he was thankful that no one was injured, and no blame was to be placed for the fire.

Dad made a call to Jesse and Red Robertson on the same day. Jesse and Red were carpenters from Lawton, and they sure did know how to make the sawdust fly. Every person who worked for the park pitched in along with other volunteers from the community and started removing the rubble while searching for any artifact that might not have burned, but almost none remained. The Park was scheduled to open for the season in sixteen days. Bob Kirk was also an excellent carpenter and between him, Jesse, Red, and forty or more workers, reconstruction quickly began. Mom, Dad, and Annie started ordering more inventory from traders in New Mexico and Arizona, Brice Privette at Pawnee Bill's Indian Trading Post, John Frank at Frankoma Pottery, and other sources.

The Lawton Constitution reported that construction progress was moving along almost as fast as the building had been razed by fire. Electricians, painters, and decorators completed their work at a record pace. Mamo oversaw workers as they began unpacking Granddad's remaining stored keepsakes and pictures not destroyed in the fire.

The day of the Park's opening, only sixteen days later, a larger and more beautiful Indian Curio Store opened, fully stocked and ready for business. A grand opening for the Indian Curio Store and Museum was staged, and the newspapers covered the event with front-page stories. As usual, Dad made a production out of the disaster. People said Frank Rush was the only man in Southwest Oklahoma who could accomplish the task so quickly and beautifully.

The newly finished Indian Curio Store and Museum was replenished with memorabilia not destroyed in the fire in 1955.

22.   THE MIDWAY

The ride area evolved as old rides were replaced by new rides. For example, the track for the Auto Raceway ride was replaced to make room for more kiddie rides and the train station. The Auto Raceway cars were an operational nightmare, somewhat dangerous, and took up a good bit of room.

The Auto Raceway ride.

Midge-O-Racer ride.

The Roto Whip ride.

The Bulgy the Fish ride.

The Midge-O-Racer ride.

Kiddie Rides were ten cents or 6 rides for 50 cents. Amusement rides, including a Roto-Whip, Midge-O-Racer, and Bulgy Fish were among the best and newest available during the 1940s. Each of these kiddie rides is considered a classic, and many models are still in operation today.

The original Parker Ferris Wheel ride had enclosed baskets or cages. This was a thrilling ride for its time, but it was slow to load and unload and it had to be operated with care. If the wheel was loaded out of balance, the drive cable would slip and the whole contraption would rock back and forth, giving the riders an unexpected thrill. This same ride is still in operation at the fairgrounds in Mountain View, Oklahoma.

The early day Parker Ferris Wheel Ride and colorful carousel. (left)
The Parker Ferris Wheel with lights aglow. (right)

In 1955 the Ferris Wheel was replaced with a new Rock-O-Plane ride which was more thrilling because the tubs could be made to roll upside-down by the rider, and it was a much safer high ride.

The new Rock-O-Plane ride.

A three-abreast, thirty-horse, Allan Herschell Merry-Go-Round complete with an air-driven calliope, was the centerpiece of the midway, and the music added to the atmosphere of the rides.

A typical Allan Herschell Merry-Go-Round horse.

23. TRAINS, TRAINS, TRAINS

The miniature train rides were always the most important attraction at both Craterville locations, and in years to come, at Sandy Lake Amusement Park. I use the word "trains" in plural because there was a record-breaking total of nine trains that Dad operated at the three parks.

The first train Dad purchased for Craterville Park was an Ottaway brand, steam-driven 12-gauge train. Gauge refers to the distance between rails in inches. While the little Ottaway Train Company locomotive was attractive, it had neither the capacity nor power to pull enough passengers to be profitable. It was also complicated to operate because it was powered by live steam. Dad later purchased another 12-gauge gas-powered Streamliner miniature train manufactured by The Miniature Train Company, but while it was easier to operate it was also of low capacity.

Dad's first train, an Ottoway Train Company locomotive at Craterville Park. c. 1942

101

The second train at Craterville Park was a Miniature Train Company Streamliner. c. 1944

Century Flyer trains, built by the National Amusement Device Company of Dayton, Ohio, came on the market by the mid-1940s and Dad quickly traded for a brand new one. They were gasoline-powered by a Ford Flat Head engine, a three-speed standard transmission, and had plenty of power to pull four train cars holding 32 people. The Century Flyer had a wider 24-gauge track giving it more weight and stability.

The Century Flyer was used at both old and new Craterville Park until Dad replaced it in the fall of 1961, but while in operation at each park it was a real workhorse. It hauled hundreds of thousands of customers and was a showpiece at both parks.

An aerial view of the Century Flyer showing the car names: Craterville Park Express, Oklahoma Rocket, Texas Special, and Frisco Railroad. c. 1955.

Ollie Couch, a long-time engineer at Craterville Park, announcing "ALL ABOARD!"
Notice the Rocking R brand on the front of the engine.

The train station at Craterville Park.

It is worth taking a little side trip in this train story to follow the Century Flyer through its storied history. When Craterville Park closed, the Century Flyer was moved to new Craterville Park. At about the same time Dad had purchased a new C.P. Huntington train (serial number CPH#8) to use at the Indian Curio Store in Cache. The Cache location did not have enough foot traffic to make a train profitable at that location. In 1961 the new Huntington train was moved from Cache to new Craterville Park because the old Century Flyer needed an update and replacement. I do not know who Dad sold it to, however, in the early 1970s it turned up in Hydro, Oklahoma on the grounds of the annual Hydro Free Fair. There it was only used a few days each year for about half a century. By 2019, it was still in operation but needed some TLC. At that point, the Hydro Free Fair board, led by my friend Charlie Wieland, raised funds by donation to have a restoration completed by the Meridian Technology Center in Stillwater, Oklahoma. While being refurbished Covid hit, and the Hydro Free Fair was cancelled in 2020. In 2021 the Century Flyer, looking showroom new in every respect, was again in the spotlight and continuing to thrill children and adults alike. Incidentally, the Hydro Free Fair is held annually in mid-August and is a must-see event. Ride the Century Flyer while you're there, it will be a thrill.

The pre-restoration Century Flyer oscillating headlight.

The refurbished Century Flyer at the Hydro Free Fair in 2021. with Frank Rush III driving.

While waiting to get back on track, there is more E. Frank Rush miniature train history to discover.

Story #1: When new Craterville Park opened in 1957 the same train track rails from Craterville Park were reused. As train wheels do after many years of use, in a curve, they start to wear out more on one side than the other. The train at Craterville Park ran in a counterclockwise direction and thus had a lot of wear on the righthand wheels. When the train was mounted on the same track at new Craterville Park it also ran counterclockwise. Due to the aforementioned wheel wear, it kept jumping the track. Since the train moved at a relatively slow speed no harm was done, except for the recurring aggravation of hoisting it back in place, causing lost revenue on busy days.

Dad surveyed the situation and quickly solved the problem. He told his crew to turn the train around, so it would run clockwise, at which time they questioned his soundness of mind. Sure enough, the unworn left side wheels then contacted the lefthand track. There were no more derailments. Problem solved!

Story #2: When new Craterville Park was eventually sold in 1965, CPH#8 was sold back to Chance Manufacturing. CPH#8 did not come back to my attention until September 2005. Dwayne Witchman, my friend at Chance Manufacturing, called me and told me CPH#8 was quickly resold by his company to City Park in New Orleans, Louisiana. The train had operated there for about 40 years but had been reported to be under 10 feet of flood water after Hurricane Katrina. I learned later that CPH#8 was recovered, restored, and put back in operation once again.

Story #3: Dad, and our family, owned Sandy Lake Amusement Park in Dallas, Texas from 1971 until 2018. The first ride we purchased was another new C.P. Huntington train. This one was train CPH#89. Over the next 48 years of operation at Sandy Lake Amusement Park we purchased, used, and then resold a total of 5 CPH trains. About every 10 years we would trade trains with Chance Manufacturing. Of course, the trains always had upgrades in manufacturing and safety features but they were also more expensive. Depreciation in tax savings usually made up the difference. Besides, we always had the newest model train.

Chance Manufacturing tracks the history of each of its rides. They reported six new trains sold to Dad and their later history.

#8 repurchased by Chance /resold to Old City Park, New Orleans, LA.
#89 repurchased by Chance / later scrapped by an unknown owner.
#165 repurchased by Chance /resold to Indianapolis Zoological Society.
#217 repurchased by Chance /resold to a private buyer.
#253 repurchased by Chance / resold to a park in Mexico City.
#315 was sold by Sandy Lake Amusement Park to David Frank Rush when the park closed in 2018.

Story #4: As you have just learned, in Dad's lifetime he owned and operated 9 different miniature trains. In 2019 I called my friend, Dick Chance the owner of Chance Manufacturing to ask a question. Understanding that Mr. Chance would be the most reliable source for my research I queried, "Do you know of anyone, anywhere in the amusement business that has owned and operated nine or more miniature trains other than Dad?" He replied, "No, not even close. My dad (Harold Chance, deceased founder of Chance Manufacturing) sold the St. Louis Zoo five CPH trains and five CPH trains to Forest Park in Fort Worth, Texas." Mr. Chance continued, "My records show that our company sold Frank six C.P. Huntington trains. My dad (Dick Chance) also sold your dad one Ottaway train in 1942. Mr. Rush also owned an MTRC Streamliner and a NAD Century Flyer plus six of ours making a total of 9 trains owned by one operator, Mr. Rush. That is, without question, an industry record."

Pictures of the six C.P. Hunting trains Dad owned.

    The midway had another ride to explore. The Fly-O-Plane ride was Manufactured by the Eyerly Aircraft Company. Eyerly originally designed a similar machine named the Orientator to teach pilots how to fly, then adopted a version for use in amusement parks. Initially called the Acroplane, the newly renamed Fly-O-Plane was a thriller, so Dad replaced the Auto Raceway with a brand-new model in 1949. The ride had eight two-seat "tubs" designed to resemble a real airplane. Once the ride started to rotate a cable system raised the tubs to about 25 feet in height at which point the passengers could steer the wings causing the simulated airplane to either fly level or corkscrew as it sped in a circle. The ride was nicknamed "The Vomit Comet" and it lived up to its reputation quite often.

A cautious young customer inspects the Fly-O-Plane.

A sizeable crowd watches a live performance on the stage in the background with the Fly-O-Plane in the foreground. The old Auto Raceway tack served perfectly as a runway for the new Fly-O-Plane.

Gastronomic delights have always been part of the attraction of amusement parks. Craterville Park offered a full menu including ice cold "sodepop," cotton candy, hand-cut ice cream sandwiches, farm-fresh salted peanuts, and "Real Root Beer" to name a few.

The early-day Refreshment Stand located in the heart of the midway.

A new modern refreshment stand opened in 1951.

24. THE OLD SWIMMING HOLE

The Craterville Park Pool was legendary. The big spring-fed swimming pool lay along Crater Creek about a half-mile north of the center of the park. Back then, there were fewer requirements for safety. Lifeguards patrolled the pool, in addition, a sign stated, "Not responsible for accidents. The owner." In those days that was enough to protect against liability. Rarely did an injury occur, but when they did band-aids and "monkey blood" (iodine) was available. The pool was a few hundred feet in length and lay below a concrete dam that had been built in the early 1930s. You could dive or jump into the water from granite boulders up to thirty feet above water level. The water was held in the pool by a small concrete wall with a sluice gate creating a shallow children's pool.

There were dressing rooms with swimsuit rentals and a small refreshment stand serving cold drinks and snacks. The water was reasonably clear most of the time but contained no chemicals. It mattered little if you quenched your thirst with a sip or two. There were fish, turtles, frogs, and an occasional snake in the water. People gave the critters little notice because it was a natural pool and a wonderful place to spend a summer day.

This 1930s photo of the upper dam and swimming pool features the slide and a standing-room-only crowd.

By the 1950s, when this pool picture was taken, swimming attire had made some noticeable changes.

Being spring-fed, the water was reasonably clear and chilly in the Craterville Park Pool.

Besides being a fairly good fishing lake, turtles, frogs and an occasional snake made for some extra excitement.

Not much had changed when Vickie and I visited the pool in February of 2024.

Located between the pool and the park were cabins, mostly of cobblestone and wood frame construction, a few of which were the residences of previous owners. Granddad added to or remodeled cabins over time. In the early years, the cabins were rented as a revenue stream. Over time the cabins were used more by park employees. Dad would hire people and give them a free place to live, which was an important benefit. The employees enjoyed living at the park, and Dad knew they would always be near at hand when he needed them.

This 2024 photo shows the only cabin left standing. Located just north of the Rush Inn Restaurant building, this cabin was mostly concrete.

In 2024, this cobblestone and concrete bench waits patiently for someone in need of a place to rest beside the road to the Craterville Park Swimming Pool.

25. IT'S SHOWTIME

The show stage was the center of the park attractions, both physically and figuratively. The stage was an elevated platform 60 feet square complete with lights and a sound system. During the 34 years Craterville Park existed, more celebrities and specialty acts performed here than any other single place in southwest Oklahoma. In all but one instance the shows were free. There was no parking fee, no purchase or pass required, and no obligation to spend a dime at the park.

Without question, the most notable celebrity was Roy Rogers. By coincidence, Roy's personal manager for over four decades was Dad's distant cousin Art Rush. Dad wanted Roy to make a personal appearance at the park. The arrangements were made for Trigger and Roy to perform and sign autographs on July 4, 1946. Roy had just finished a show in Chicago, and he and Trigger were flying to their next show in New Orleans. Roy, Trigger, and the Sons of the Pioneers landed at the airport in Lawton. Trigger flew with Roy in a specially built stall on the plane. The plane's arrival in Lawton was kept secret to prevent a swarm of people from coming to the airport.

"Whoa Trigger," as they say. There was a problem of major proportions. Some souvenir hunters in Chicago had found Trigger unattended and cut his tail off. Not the whole tail, but the hair had been bobbed off. Trigger's appearance would have had to be canceled but for the quick thinking of Art Rush. He called RKO studios in California and had a false tail flown in. The tress arrived in Lawton about the same time Roy and Trigger landed. It was braided into place, and the audience never knew the difference.

Roy Rogers, Trigger, and The Sons of the Pioneers appeared on the Craterville Park stage in 1946 drawing the largest crowd in the history of the park.

Roy Rogers, Trigger, and a lady band member left Lawton airport with a fawn which was a gift for Roy. (Roy and Dale Evans were not married until 1947.)

Roy Rogers was a superstar at the height of his popularity when he appeared at Craterville Park in 1946. This was the only time an admission fee was charged at the park and the settlement paper for Roy and Dad's fifty-fifty split, after expenses, is shown below on park letterhead. Roy was the headliner, but other stage acts, the band, and fireworks were part of the celebration. The biggest expense was the airplane ride for Trigger.

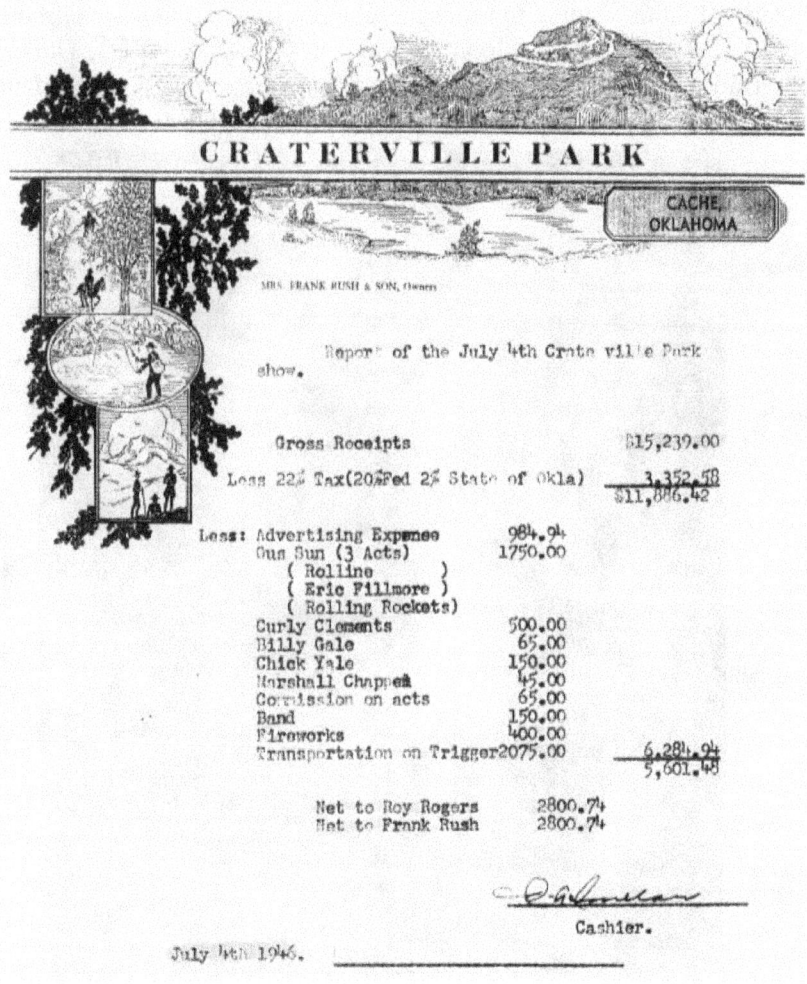

The Roy Rogers settlement sheet, July 4, 1946.

Other famous stars from television, movies, and the Grand Ole Opry often made special guest appearances at Craterville Park. Singers included Roy Acuff, Homer and Jethro, Grandpaw Jones, Little Jimmie Dickens, and the duo Lester Flat and Earl Scruggs. Western movie stars including Tex Ritter, Montie Montana, and Rex Allen drew capacity crowds. Duncan Renaldo, a.k.a. The Cisco Kid, performed and became a close friend of Dad's.

Duncan fell in love with Craterville Park and told Dad, in all sincerity, that he wanted to retire there. Even though Duncan retired in 1956, the Land Grab was looming, so it never came to pass. Duncan sent Dad and Mom Christmas cards and letters every year until he passed away in 1980.

The Cisco Kid and his beautiful mount Diablo appear in a publicity photo signed, "To my dear friend, Frankie. (That's me).

Rex Allen was booked as part of the annual Independence Day Celebration in 1954. Rex appeared in a score of Western movies. He had several hit records in the genre of "Western music," as well as songs that became standards in popular music including "Crying in the Chapel". He did shows at both Craterville Park and later at new Craterville Park.

An advertisement poster announcing Rex Allen's appearance on July 3rd and 4th, 1954. Fireworks and all of the park's amenities were on the bill.

Rex was waiting in our home for a couple of hours before showtime at the park. Rex asked Mom about her piano and if she played, and she said she did. He got his guitar out of its case, tuned it, and asked Mom to accompany him on her piano. Mom could play "by ear" and was familiar with his music. He sang several of his most popular tunes, including "The Streets of Laredo". That was a real treat for Mom.

Handsome and colorful Rex Allen was a big hit, especially with Mom.

Television was young in the early 1950s, but people starring in the TV series were already celebrities. The Grand Ole Opry and country and western music were widely listened to on radio. Western movies at local theaters were probably the most popular entertainment for kids and adults. To gain recognition and make a good wage, the stars of these media made public appearances in about any suitable venue. Craterville Park was an ideal setting during the warmer months of the year.

The question of why Craterville Park became so popular might hinge on a few facts. For example, events like the Easter Pageant at the Holy City in the Wichita Mountains drew a large crowd, but it was a once-a-year occurrence. Rodeos and circuses in Lawton and other surrounding cities were much the same. Few venues could hold several hundred or a few thousand people. Another obvious fact was there were no multi-screen movie theaters or professional sports in the area. Until about 1950, television was not widely available and there were only four channels at the most. People were hungry for wholesome family entertainment, thus, personal appearances kept the park marketable.

Younger generations may not fully understand why some of the celebrities mentioned in the book are significant. If you lived during that time and got to visit Craterville Park, get a personal autographed photo, and meet these iconic superstars, it would be a lifelong memory.

Red Foley was a major influence on country music after World War II, recording dozens of top hits including "Tennessee Saturday Night."

Ernest Tubb recorded 58 number-one country hits including "Waltz Across Texas", often played as a classic song today.

Porter Wagoner was famous for his blonde pompadour hairstyle, his flashy "Nudie" rhinestone suits, and at least 50 hit songs including "Satisfied Mind", "Green, Green Grass of Home", and "Just Between You and Me."

"The Midnight Cowboy," Bill Mack, performed at the park numerous times. He wrote the song "Blue" made famous by LeAnn Rimes, and "Drinking Champagne", another hit song recorded by several artists. Bill's 45-rpm record of "Fat Woman" and "Milk Cow Blues" was not nearly as popular, however, he sold and signed a lot of copies when he visited Craterville Park.

Bill Mack, singer, songwriter, and also known as the "Midnight Cowboy" on his *All Night Truckers Show* on the radio.

Carl Smith's best songs including "Hey, Joe!" and "There She Goes."

Roy Acuff the iconic
"King of Country Music."

"Cousin" Minnie Pearl, a comedian with her
familiar "HOWDEEE!" greeting.

Johnny Horton's best songs were
"North to Alaska" and "The Battle of New Orleans."

Stonewall Jackson's biggest hits were
"Waterloo" and "Life to Go."

Dale Robertson starred in the TV series
Wagon Train, as well as *Iron Horse,* and *Death Valley Days.*

Jimmy Wakley was best known for his songs
"Silver Bells" and "A Bushel and a Peck."

James Brown (no, not THAT James Brown)
Star of TV series *Rip Masters and Rin Tin Tin*.

Marty Robbins had 94 recordings on
the country charts including "El Paso."

George "Gabby" Hayes was the movie "sidekick" to Roy Rogers and John Wayne and scores of other "B" westerns.

Dad's receipt books show that the fee charged for most personal appearances was "Paid in Cash" in the amount of $250. More popular stars commanded $750, an amount that wouldn't begin to interest any top artist today.

By the time Tex Ritter performed at Craterville Park in 1956, he had appeared on Broadway, starred in 70 movies, and written and recorded several iconic western songs including the 1953 Oscar-winning song "The Ballad of High Noon." It is not an understatement to count him as one of the most revered stars of that era.

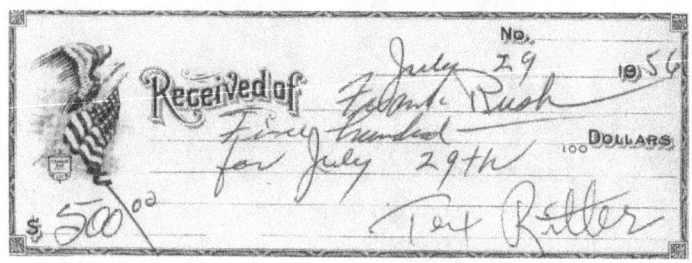

The $500 handwritten receipt for Tex Ritter's appearance was paid by check and acknowledged by Tex himself.

Souvenir photo of Tex Ritter and his horse White Flash.

    The Craterville Park Express was a working stagecoach and served as an autograph platform for the stars. The stars were seated atop the coach allowing onlookers a better photo opp. The steps allowed excited fans to get close to their idols, and at the same time keep them from mobbing the celebrity. The stars furnished their own souvenir 8x10 publicity photos, and almost without exception, signed autographs until everyone received a free copy.

The Craterville Park Express stagecoach.

26. AMAZING ACTS

Over the years, there were many famous circus acts, including a high diver who dived from a 120-foot-tall tower into a tank filled with only six feet of water. Performers included trapeze artists, bicycle trick riders, and a very attractive lady named LaLage performed a somewhat racy (for that time) aerial act.

The troop of bicycle trick riders could ride anything on wheels. They had the world's tallest unicycle at twenty feet, a bicycle built for ten upon which all members of the family rode, and a tiny bike that was only eight inches tall. The entire family was very talented, especially the four voluptuous female members of the troop whose main contribution was to pose along the edge of the stage encouraging the audience to applaud. The ladies were dressed in costumes, but "WowWee" what costumes! They left "almost nothing" to the imagination. While the men in the crowd were concentrating on "almost nothing," the cyclists performed their variety of tricks. I was a young lad at the time, but I still think that was the most memorable act that ever came to Craterville Park.

There were trained dogs and monkeys, a lion tamer, and a bear trainer. The bear trainer appeared several seasons at the park, but shortly after his final visit, he met an untimely end in Kansas City. Missouri. We learned that one of the bears had cornered and killed him in his truck-mounted steel cage.

The most heart-stopping act and the most dangerous were the Sky Kings. They performed on four one hundred-foot poles set up in a square pattern about forty feet apart and with brace wires running to the ground. Atop the braced portion of the poles were thirty-foot flexible mast poles on which four men performed acrobatic moves as the poles swayed back and forth under their weight. The song "Cherry Pink and Apple Blossom White" was the perfect match for the tempo of the swaying poles. For a finale, the Sky Kings would swap poles in mid-air. The fearless move was met by roaring applause from the crowd. The act visited both parks and at one juncture during the pole change at new Craterville Park, two of the four performers accidentally wound up on the same pole. The combined weight of both men could have snapped the spring steel pole had they not quickly descended to the relative safety of the braced section. No one was harmed, but the crowd cheered even louder, thinking it was part of the act.

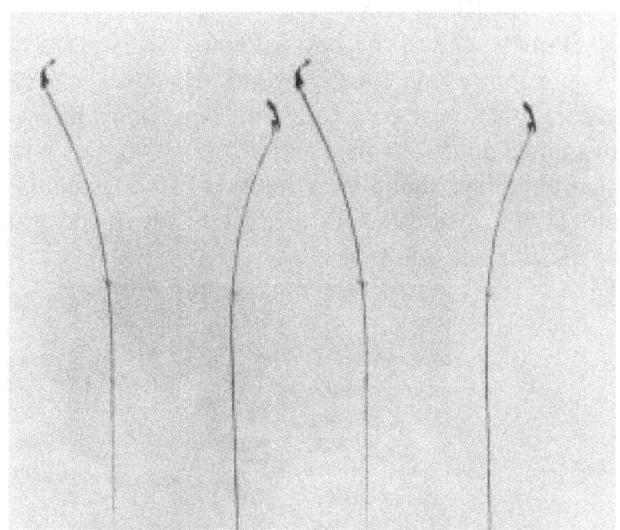

The Sky Kings Sway Pole Act with the performers doing a handstand.

Hugo, the Human Cannon Ball, was fired, body and soul, from a truck-sized cannon into a suspended catch net some three hundred feet away. He never missed the net, but his life insurance policy had a special disclaimer attached. Hugo's wife was responsible for the control buttons inside the truck, and on one occasion she pulled the trigger slightly before Hugo was ready. Hugo wasn't happy even though he was not injured. Mrs. Hugo just laughed and said it gave a whole new meaning to the term "ready or not."

Hugo the Human Cannon Ball flying high above a crowd.

Bobo Barnett, one of the best-known clowns of all time, made at least two appearances at Craterville Park. He had a very small, battery-operated car, in which he could cram his large body, baggy clothes, and a pack of trained dogs. The best part of the act was his arrival on stage. No one could believe that a large man and 10 dogs could fit into such cramped quarters inside the little car. His antics and trained canines were fun for kids and adults alike.

Funny man, Bobo Barnett.

Circus clown, Chuck Yale.

This is by no means all of the acts that performed at Craterville Park.

Musical groups were popular. On one occasion Ernest Tubb returned to the park for an encore performance including his famous band, "The Texas Troubadours."

"The Jubilee Promenaders."

Curley Clements and the "Rodeo Rangers."

Billie Gayle's "Hollywood Cowgirls."

"The Early Bird Band," stars on WFAA radio in Dallas, Texas.

Craterville Park even held an annual
"Miss Craterville Park Beauty Pageant."

Miss Craterville Park.

By today's standards, drawing a crowd like this doesn't look especially impressive, but this was a sizable gathering back in the day. Visiting Craterville Park on a Saturday or Sunday, enjoying a free show, and likely running into your friends and neighbors was a day well spent.

27.   INDIAN POWWOWS

Granddad's cultivation of his relationship with Indian tribes started before moving to the Wichita Mountains. While living and working on ranches in the Osage country of Northern Oklahoma, he gained the friendship of the Osage tribal leaders of that area.

Comanche Chief Quanah Parker and other tribal leaders and their families were quick to hold Granddad in high esteem for his part in orchestrating the return of the buffalo. One can imagine how the news surrounding Granddad's trip to New York and the euphoria of seeing live buffalo return to the plains acted to raise his stature. Once he and the Comanche, Kiowa, and Apache leaders became closely acquainted, they revered him as an ally concerned for their causes and well-being.

There are numerous accounts of Granddad taking on Indian affairs as his own. He spoke before congressional committees and the state legislature of Oklahoma championing their concerns and testifying on their behalf.

On a personal note, in the movie *McClintock,* John Wayne is portrayed speaking on behalf of the Indian tribes and protesting their forced relocation to "this place you call Fort Sill." I can relate to the tribal chiefs entrusting their white friend, George Washington McClintock, to interpret their wishes just as they did Granddad.

It is probable, that Granddad was one of the few white people who genuinely cared about and counseled his Indian friends regarding their defeat and forced assimilation from the late 1800s and the formative years of the early 1900s.

For millennium, Indians populated the ancient mountains as well as the treasured site which became the Township of Craterville. Artifacts and evidence of their presence indicate they favored the attributes of this exact location. Although there is little ancient documented history, a good place to camp remains a good place to camp, especially in these granite hills that seemingly never change.

In the years leading up to 1923, informal powwows occurred in and near the Craterville Park site, mostly for the tribe's personal purposes. As progress would have it, once the location became an enterprise, park visitors started gathering to watch. Granddad scheduled and advertised powwows with dancing contests and a structured format for years to come. Granddad did not invent powwows, but he did advance them as organized and scheduled public events.

The powwows at Craterville Park were amazing. To be sure, they were not the tribal rituals of days long past, nor were they the often-diluted staged events we know today. They were celebratory events, and those Indian families enjoyed the moment. The songs were a concert of jubilation. The drummers usually were also the singers, and the music was haunting yet invigorating. The regalia of the plains Indians were generally more flamboyant than those of other tribes and each dancer had his or her unique design. The exquisite beadwork, featherwork, eagle bones, elk teeth, bells, shells, and horsehair were lovingly and traditionally designed, usually by close family members. Dust kicking and verbal yelps served as an expression of a dancer's interpretation. The Fast War Dance, Fancy War Dance, Eagle Dance, Hoop Dance, Round Dance, and Friendship Dances were only some of the standards. Once the colors, cadence, and melodies worked their way into the spectator's mind and heart, they consumed the senses. Many times, at Craterville Park, we would awaken as the sun was rising and hear the chants of the singers as they ended a long night of social dancing.

What started as a social event primarily for the Indians grew into a real tourist attraction. Before the early days whites were not often invited nor were they particularly interested in tribal gatherings. I can promise Granddad recognized what he was a witness to, and this was smack in the middle of his wheelhouse when it came to engaging locals and tourists alike.

Granddad called on a group of tribal leaders including Horse, Buffalo, Sauppetty, George Cable, and others, to join him in organizing an "agricultural Indian fair." The group wished to give continuity and credence to the event. On May 25, 1924, The Craterville Park Covenant was signed by thumbprint of the tribal leaders and Granddad's signature. Horse races, traditional Indian sports, crafts, Indian dance contests, and many other contests were held as part of the event with Indian judges elected by tribe members.

Granddad with the Craterville Covenant. c.1924.

The Craterville Park Covenant was hand-painted on tanned deer hide. The Indian chiefs signed by thumbprint.
Granddad signed by script.

The Craterville Park Covenant. This covenant made and entered into by Frank Rush of Craterville Park, Comanche County Oklahoma, Party of the first part, and the Indians whose names are subscribed, party of the second part. Witnessth: it has become necessary for the American Indians to take steps for the advancement and uplift of their people and especially to teach their children the value of building character and becoming self supporting, this covenant is entered into as a means towards that end. Therefore, the parties hereto covenant and agree among themselves as follows, There shall be held annually at Craterville Park an agricultural Indian Fair. The object of this fair will be to create self evidence and to encourage leadership by the Indian for his people, a belief in the capacity of the Indian to better his position and to take his place on terms of equality with other races in the competitive pursuits of every day life, and a desire to accomplish the most possible for himself and his people. All Officers, Directors, Judges and Exhibitors at the aforesaid fair must be Indians, all said Officers, Directors and Judges must be elected by the Indians themselves. In Testimony, whereof we have hereunto set our hands this 25th day of May, 1924.
Horse, Buffalo, Sauppetty, Geo. Cable, Frank Rush
Written By, Freddie Dee

The text of The Craterville Covenant.

A rare group photograph of the principal tribal leaders at the Craterville Park Indian Powwow. c. 1928.

Signers of the Craterville Covenant. c. 1924

Granddad with Indians in ceremonial dress, May 25, 1924.

As the fair grew in attendance and stature, the principal tribes represented became better organized. One major step, under Granddad's guidance, was the forming of a corporation titled The

Craterville Park Oklahoma State Indian Fair Association. It was filed and granted in the spring of 1928. The signatories were Big Bow of Carnegie, Chief Millett of Geronimo, Hunting Horse of Meers, Ned E. Brace of Carnegie, Herman Asenap of Indiahoma, Enoch Smokey of Verden, Oscar Yellow Wolf of Cache, and Tennyson Berry of Fort Cobb, all residents of Oklahoma. This original document, issued by the Oklahoma Department of State, was presented to Granddad for safekeeping. Owing to the fact that it hung in the park's office at old Craterville Park, it did not burn in the 1955 museum fire.

The original Craterville Park Oklahoma State Indian Fair Association Certificate of Incorporation signed June 8, 1928.

Granddad planned an Editors Day at Craterville Park. Tribal members, dressed in full regalia, and newspaper editors were invited to witness and report the announcement of the formation of the corporation.

The announcers stand at an early Oklahoma State Indian Fair. c. 1930.

An Indian parade passes for review at the grandstands in the Exhibit Pasture at Craterville Park.

An advertising poster from 1932.

Craterville Park Oklahoma State Indian Fair was staged in the Exhibit Pasture. This view is looking north with grandstands on the left and dust is rising from a horse race on the track in the distance. c. 1930s.

Two Indians and a cowboy. The real deal.

The last official Indian Fair was held at Craterville Park on August 25, 26 and 27, 1932. Members of 14 tribes were present, and a crowd numbering thousands attended. Will Rogers, the famous actor and columnist of Cherokee Indian descent, was also present. The Indian Fair was a monumental success.

In early 1933, through an amicable agreement, Indian tribes chose to move the official fair to a permanent home on tribal land in Anadarko, Oklahoma, and it was renamed the American Indian Exposition.

Granddad passed away later that year, but Dad continued to hold powwows each year until the park was displaced in the Land Grab in 1957. Craterville Park powwows continued to draw large crowds and were favored by Indian families because of tradition, their relationship with Dad, and the picturesque setting.

Colorful Indian dancers pose for a Lawton Constitution newspaper story. George "Woogie" Watchetaker was awarded the coveted title of World Champion Fancy War Dancer three times. Tribal leader Edgar Monetatchi Sr. (center) was the master of ceremonies for several years at Craterville Park Powwows. Edgar's son. is also shown.

28. CRATERVILLE PARK RODEOS

The rodeo grounds were located to the east of the main complex of Craterville Park in the Exhibition Pasture. Granddad started producing rodeos on the Fourth of July in 1924, and grandstands that would hold a few thousand people were erected.

At first, the rodeo contestants were local cowboys, and there wasn't an arena fence. People pulled their cars up in a big circle and the action took place in the open space in the center. Events included wild cow riding rather than bull riding. When saddle broncs were ridden, the cowboys mounted bucking horses in the middle of the arena without the aid of bucking chutes. Two hazing horses crowded the bronc between them, and a hazer placed a flour sack over the bronc's eyes to quiet the animal. The contestant climbed over the back of a hazing horse and down onto the saddle. Quickly, the hazer pulled the sack from the horse's eyes, and the cowboy tried to ride the horse until it quit bucking. To attract the attention of the judges, a bronc rider might flog his mount with his hat as an act of bravado. Cowboys had respect for the animal's ability. Once a cowboy was safely on the ground, and after an especially good effort on the part of his mount, a cowboy might tip his hat in salute to the animal.

"Earing" down a tough one before side gate bucking chutes were used.

As the sport progressed in the calf roping and steer roping events, front-opening roping chutes came into use. Similarly, side-release bucking chutes for the bucking events were updated improvements. There were no bucking bulls, trophy buckles, or ceremonies at first, just prize money and bragging rights, but times were changing. New contest rules and innovations were being introduced in rodeos, and the popularity of the sport was growing as a result.

In later years, modern side-release bucking chutes were added. Cowboys and soldiers from Fort Sill watch the action.

Dad hired a famous rodeo announcer and producer named Foghorn Clancy to help add color and structure to the rodeo. Foghorn used only a megaphone to announce the events and his booming voice carried to the far corners of the grandstands.

Cowboys such as Windy Ryon, Todd Whatley, Freckles Brown, and Buck Rutherford from Texas and Oklahoma entered to show their talents and win the jackpots. Grand entry flags, a rodeo band, and specialty acts were added, and the crowds grew each year.

Foghorn Clancy.

The Exhibition Pasture Grandstand was used for both Indian powwows and rodeos.

The grandstands offered convenient concessions.

Many of the specialty acts and contestants, some listed below in the rodeo advertisement, would eventually be recognized as honorees by the Rodeo Cowboy Hall of Fame and other prestigious organizations.

155

There was a lot of action advertised in a full-page newspaper ad for the 1940 rodeo and Independence Day celebration.

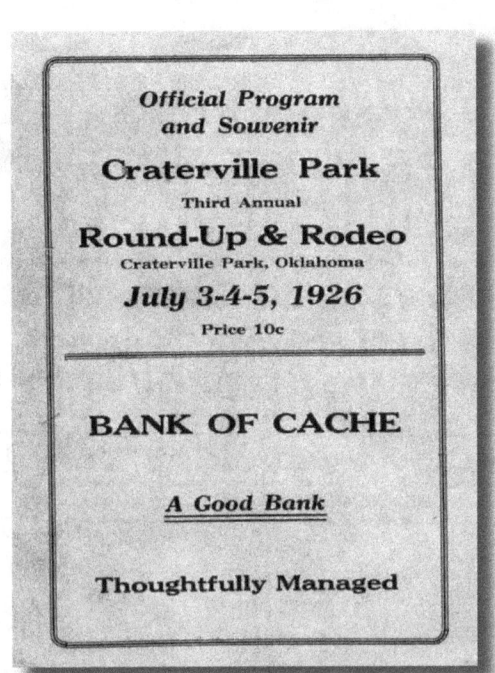

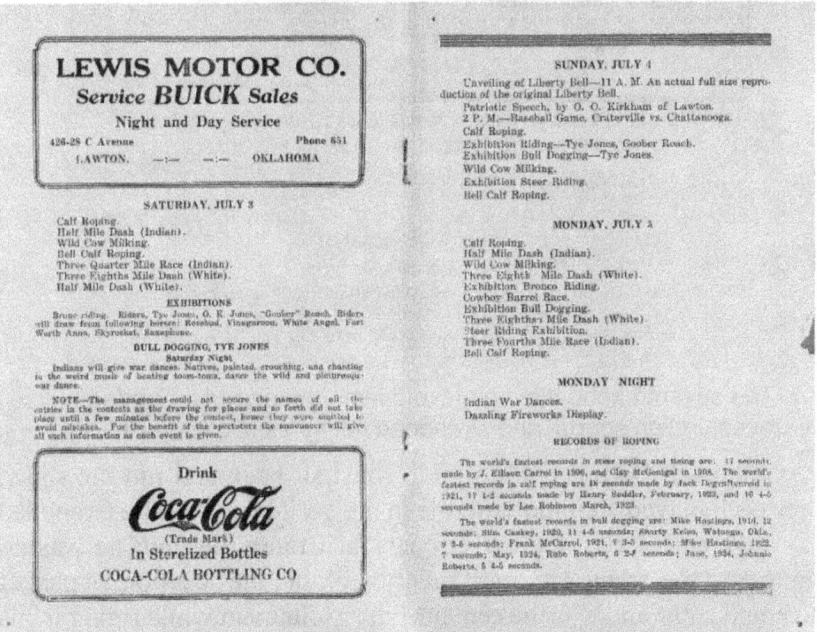

The 1926 program for the Third Annual Craterville Park Round-Up and Rodeo.

The seventh annual event advertisement featured the rodeo, horse races, Indian sports, and Granddad riding his "Cowboy Chariot."

    Granddad, Dad, and Mom didn't just sit back and run the show. They each played an important role in the excitement. While Granddad was alive and during the early rodeos at Craterville Park he was no stranger to the arena. He traditionally took his introduction as part of the grand entry and was the center of the excitement while riding in his Cowboy Chariot. A wild buffalo was cinched to the arched chariot tongue by a swiveling hitch. Granddad Rush held on as the buffalo was released and charged around the arena to the cheers of the crowd. If the buffalo turned to charge, the chariot was kept just out of reach by the arched tongue. What could possibly go wrong?

RODEO & RACES
July 3, 4, 5 — Craterville Park
15 Miles West of Lawton

Granddad's Cowboy Chariot was pulled by a feral longhorn steer or a wild buffalo. In either case, there was no steering wheel. If the animal ran toward the chariot he could never get close enough to make contact. Hopefully!

Fagon Miller, a young boy from Odell, Texas, had come to the park on a family vacation and he got to following Dad around. Fagon was a ranch-raised cowboy and could handle any chore with horses or cattle. Dad put him to work in the park, and he started milking cows at the barn to earn extra money. Fagon also worked with the saddle horse string. He and Dad bought a pair of horses and decided they wanted to learn to trick ride. There was a lady named Teddy Jacobs and her sister from Wills Point, Texas, who came to ride in the women's bronc riding and perform their trick riding act. Dad saw no reason to hire an outside act when the Jacobs sisters, Fagon, and he could do the job. They had some custom trick riding saddles built at Oliver Saddle Shop in Vernon, Texas, and taught themselves to do all the tricks the rodeo professionals could do. Dad and Fagon got very skilled as they practiced. In addition, "Trick riding is a lot more glamorous than milking cows," according to Fagon.

One home movie of Dad trick riding at a Craterville Park rodeo shows him doing a tail stand on Tony, his trick-riding horse, as they sped down the arena. It was a risky trick, which not all trick riders would attempt. The tail stand required him to hold on to the cruppers or handles at the rear of the saddle and do a headstand with his head down by the horse's tail and his body vertically above. Mom always said the reason Dad complained about a sore neck was because he fell off hitting the ground headfirst. Mom recalled, "He bounced three or four times on his head, just like a pogo stick with arms."

E. Frank Rush performing a shoulder stand on his speeding horse Tony in front of the crowd and the giant loudspeaker horns at a Craterville Park rodeo. c. 1940.

Mother had purchased a gorgeous black high school (trick) horse named Ace of Spades. He was jet black and stood sixteen hands (64 inches) tall at the withers. Ace was a cross between a Standard Bred and Tennessee Walker, and he was an eyeful. Mom recalled how everything about Ace said, "Look at me." He was trained for dressage work as well as circus stunts, so Mom developed her specialty act for the rodeo. Back then, people didn't get much of a chance to see show horses of Ace's quality or ability. Mom's skill as an equestrian with Ace of Spades and other horses was apparent. Mom had a natural seat in the saddle or as horsemen say, "she could sit a horse." Dad always said she and Ace were the biggest hit at the rodeos.

Genelle Rush and Ace of Spades saluted the crowd at a Craterville Park Rodeo.

One of the many popular features of the Craterville Park rodeos was live music. To fill that need, Dad hired the Oklahoma State Reformatory Band from Granite, Oklahoma. The inmates and their music were considered a new dimension in rodeo performances, and apparently, they were very talented, owing to the fact they had plenty of time to practice.

The popularity of the Cowboy Band from the Oklahoma State Reformatory in Granite, Oklahoma was a big asset to the rodeos.

Major Fred W. Pike, director of Oklahoma State Reformatory Cowboy Band was featured in a 1941 Lawton Constitution news article. KSWO radio in Lawton broadcasts the rodeos live at each performance.

Many of the rodeos Dad produced while owning and managing Craterville Park after Granddad passed away, were in other towns across southwest Oklahoma and north central Texas. He produced some of the earliest rodeos at Childress and Graham, Texas, along with Temple, Waurika, and Hobart Oklahoma, among others. The Childress, Texas newspaper reported on July 19, 1938, and the headline read, "CELEBRATION TERMED A COMPLETE SUCCESS." A quote from the story stated, "The rodeo contest, directed by Frank Rush Jr. (Dad) without doubt the best ever staged here. Seventy-nine cowboys competed and were awarded $1,100 in prize money."

A rodeo program announcing The Frontier Circus at Graham, Texas.

One benefit of producing rodeos at other locations was the awareness created about the rodeos at Craterville Park. Dad was a master of getting the stories out, and a sampling of the numerous news stories, which local newspapers gladly ran, proves the point. The Review in Apache, Oklahoma ran a front-page story on June 27, 1940, announcing and praising the upcoming July 3rd and 4th Rodeo at Craterville Park. A quote from the Cement Field News, Cement Oklahoma on July 29, 1940, exclaimed, "Many of the stars from years gone by will be on hand and a good many new stars will compete.... outlaw bucking horses, wild longhorn steers, and vicious Brahma bucking steers.... a mad melee of western sports with thrills coming thick and fast." News coverage like this guaranteed an overflow crowd, and each visitor got their money's worth.

In addition to performing at the Craterville Rodeos, the Reformatory Cowboy Band went on the road with Dad when he booked rodeos in nearby towns in Oklahoma. Here the group joined the Temple, Oklahoma Rodeo Parade, and then performed at the Temple Rodeo that evening.

Mom and Dad posing for a publicity photo.

29. THE RODEO SHOWDOWN

In 1936, a group of cowboys threatened to walk out, or strike, during a rodeo in the Boston Garden in Massachusetts if their entry fee was not added back into the prize money. The group's goal was to improve the money paid and other conditions such as rodeo livestock selection. The group called themselves the Cowboys' Turtle Association. Rodeo history tells us the rodeo cowboys used the word "turtle" in their title because officials had been "slow as turtles" to act on their demands. Dad joined and paid his dues as member number 1410.

Frank Rush's Cowboy's Turtle Association card.

In 1943, just before the rodeo grand entry at the Craterville Park was to get underway, and with the grandstands full of people, the cowboy contestants threatened to strike. They told Dad they wanted even more money added to the advertised prize money or they would not ride. Dad got hopping mad and told them they had made a deal, and they should stick to it. After all, he was also a CTA member. He had supported them with the issue of the entry fees being added to the prize money, but he didn't like the idea that they were threatening a strike if they didn't get more money than advertised. There was a confrontation, and the cowboys not only threatened to leave but to do a little damage to Dad and the rodeo arena on the way out.

As usual, Dad had hired the Cowboy Band from the Oklahoma State Reformatory to perform and provide music for the show. The band members were prisoners on trustee status, and between them and four armed guards, they were a formidable group. The head guard could see that the cowboys had Dad up a tree and motioned him to come over to the bandstand. Dad said the guard told him to stay next to the band, and they would see that no harm came to him. Cowboys have a reputation, occasionally deserved, for enjoying a good fight. The contestants would have, no doubt, upheld the tradition had it not been for the reformatory band.

Dad agreed to pay the extra prize money to avoid a strike. The show went on as scheduled, but he never again produced a professional rodeo. The old Cowboys' Turtle Association became the Rodeo Cowboys Association (RCA) in 1945 and in 1975 was renamed the Professional Rodeo Cowboys Association (PRCA). Dad had hard feelings against some of the early-day cowboys, but most of them remained his lifelong friends. He never lost his love for the sport.

The rodeos at Craterville Park never lost their appeal, however, the entertainment at the park was evolving. The rodeo arena was located about a half mile to the east, and not close to the heart of the park. By the early 1940s, Dad started booking specialty acts, movie stars, and Grand Ole Opry stars on the performance stage right in the middle of the park. The big performance stage had lights, a sound system, and a grass lawn that provided plenty of standing and sitting room. This move spelled the end of the rodeo business for the time being. In time, a fire almost destroyed the grandstand making it unusable, so the site was cleared for other uses.

30. DRAWING A CROWD

By now you may understand why Craterville Park was such a well-known attraction. There was hardly a week that went by that there wasn't a news story for a front-page feature in the Lawton Constitution and Morning Press, a newscast on KSWO radio, or the other media around Southwest Oklahoma. Dad paid for a good amount of advertisement, but he knew that if there was a good news story to go along with the purchase, an editor would gladly run the story.

Dad recognized creating news for people to talk about would bring in the crowds and the money. That is precisely why everything Dad learned from Granddad and almost everything his resourceful mind created could be turned into news. Most events were planned but some presented themselves as unexpected opportunities. We're going to talk about some of those stories.

An early model pickup was used for livery services around the park, and often used in local parades.

31. AROUND THE WORLD

Dad's friend Bill Wilkerson, a native Oklahoman and a Cherokee Indian, owned the Indian Store concession at Disneyland in California. Bill was also a movie character actor, mostly in roles that required an authentic-looking Indian chief. Bill had a lot of contacts in Hollywood, including a filmmaker named Lou Borzage. In late 1954, Lou was searching for locations for the buffalo stampede, Indian camp, and train scenes for Jules Verne's *Around the World In 80 Days*. Bill put Lou in touch with Dad, and the Rocking R Ranch at Craterville Park was scouted. The Exhibition Pasture was perfect for the Indian camp scene and a scene where the train was delayed by a herd of buffalo crossing a railroad track.

Some interesting trivia surrounds this event. Mike Todd was the famed owner of Todd-AO Productions, and Todd was also the producer and co-director of this highly acclaimed movie. Todd became more noted because *Around the World in 80 Days* won the Academy Award for Best Picture in 1956. At the same time, Todd was romancing film star Elizabeth Taylor and their tumultuous relationship was the lead story in every tabloid of the day, which added to the excitement.

Big equipment trucks started rolling in a few days before the actual filming. Dad had arranged for about two hundred Indians to be dressed in costumes and act as seconds. Tepees were set in place as background for the scene. The beautiful granite hills, oak trees, and all the Indian camp trappings made an outstanding setting. The Indian camp was reminiscent of bygone days, and the behind-the-scenes action made for great excitement among the locals.

The wardrobe crew passed out fake but authentic-looking bows, arrows, war clubs, shields, and all manner of Indian gear. The Indians had their own costumes, but some of them wore eyeglasses and had modern haircuts. The eyeglasses had to go, and the wardrobe department issued long, braided wigs to the Indians who needed them.

The days of preparation were long, and everyone was standing around waiting for the film crew to get set. No one complained because everyone was on the payroll at the actor's scale rate of pay, which was more money than most were used to making. Mike Todd showed up with his entourage on the day of the actual filming. Mr. Todd barked orders and made a few changes, and when finished filming he told Dad the film was exactly what he had in mind. Everyone involved cooperated and did a first class job.

MOVIE JOKE. Mike Todd impresses these Indian youths with some wild Hollywood tales before giving them hints on the technical phase of the motion picture industry. Spectators jammed the Craterville Park area Saturday afternoon to watch the movie crew and Indians in action. Many Lawtonians and Fort Sill personnel lugged their own cameras to the location. See story, page 1. (Staff Photo)

Bill Crawford's account in the Lawton Constitution recalls the filming at Craterville Park in early October 1955. Mike Todd was visiting with Indians during the filming of scenes for *Around the World in Eighty Days* at Craterville Park. Courtesy of the Lawton Constitution.

This water tower was a movie prop for *Around the World in 80 Days*. It was built on-site and left behind. After the film crew departed, Dad moved it to a prominent location near the Craterville Park railroad track so everyone visiting the park could take a picture. The sign got the movie name wrong, but few people noticed.

This photo from atop a nearby mountain shows the Indian encampment, dancers performing a round dance, and the film crew in the foreground.

The Indian camp had authentic tepees which the locals were paid to provide. I must apologize for this picture not being in color. I cannot overstate how stunning their costumes were.

The Indians were asked to return their wigs and props to the wardrobe department, which turned out to be a problem. The wardrobe manager started to take some of the personal items the Indians had brought, and the Indians claimed some of the wigs were their real hair. One Indian whooped loudly when the wardrobe man tried to remove what he thought was a wig from the man's head. The other Indians started talking in their native tongue and making threatening gestures as they surrounded the paleface. Smiling and apologizing, the shaken wardrobe man decided to let all the others turn in their wigs voluntarily. Some did but many did not. For several years following, Indians would come over to Dad at powwows, pull up their wigs, and ask jokingly, "When Mike Todd comin' back?"

32. NATIONAL GEOGRAPHIC

In 1956, Mr. Woodbridge Williams, a photographer for the National Geographic Magazine, came to Wichita Mountains and Craterville Park to take photographs for a story. In the May 1957 edition, a wonderful article, "The Wichitas—Land of the Living Prairie," gave a thorough account of the splendor of the area.

Mister Woodbridge resided at the park for several weeks while writing and taking photographs for the story. He and Dad spent hours visiting about the lore and history of the area. On a few occasions, Dad allowed me to tag along with Mister Woodbridge on his photographic journeys to the refuge. We would sit for hours in a concealed location or a portable blind with his camera at the ready, waiting for a bird or an animal to appear. At first, I was impatient. By the end of the experience, I learned to observe the detail and color of everything in view. Unexpected joy could be found in the solitude. Mister Woodbridge possessed the patience and skill necessary to take the exceptional and unusual photographs for which the magazine is known.

The National Geographic article gave Craterville Park and the refuge a big boost in notoriety.

This photo showing Bob and Alma Kirk, and Genelle and Frank Rush mounted near the refuge gate also appeared in the National Geographic article in 1957.

33.   IT'S THE LAW

Both Granddad and Dad held law enforcement officers in high regard.

Granddad lived in Blackwell, Oklahoma in 1906 while working as a ranch foreman for Pawnee Bill. While there he was appointed "Special Policeman for the Osage Reservation" by the Department of the Interior. Later, on December 30, 1909, while working at the Wichita Forest he was appointed as a Game Warden by the United States Department of Agriculture and paid $1400 per annum for his services.

At an early age, I thought most of Dad and Mom's friends were police officers. That was less true than I thought because they had lots of friends, and some did carry a badge of one agency or another. Over time, I began to understand why there were FBI agents and members of the Oklahoma Highway Patrol frequently visiting the park.

In the late 1940s, quick draw competitions became in vogue as spectator events. One reason may be the popularity of Western movies, and a second reason is survival on the part of law enforcement officers. In any event, Dad started scheduling quick draw competitions. Those events may not have been sustainable as much as powwows and rodeos, but they did have a following around the state, mostly by officers of the law. Besides, they were fun to watch.

Three lawmen who entered the competition were Weldon "Spot" Gentry and Delf A. "Jelly" Brice, both celebrated FBI agents, and Captain Dan Combs of the Oklahoma Highway Patrol. Spot was born in Lawton and Jelly was born in Mt. View, Oklahoma. Both men are nationally known in the annals of the FBI for their marksmanship and for bringing the most notorious criminals to justice dead or alive. Dan Combs was a living legend in the OHP as an exhibition shooter and supporter of the Second Amendment.

It turned out, that Spot, Jelly, and Dan, among others, developed a long-lasting friendship with Dad and Mom and often stopped by the park. Occasionally, they would stay in one of the rental cabins for a few days. Dad would always provide free room and board anytime they came. Dad said when they needed to lay low and decompress from their dangerous jobs, they knew Craterville Park was a safe haven. At our home at the Rocking R Ranch at Meers years later, Dan Combs would stay in our house and hunt with us during deer season.

OHP Captain Dan Combs.

FBI agent Jelly Bryce.

Dad and Mom both loved hunting, and each was a good shot. They decided to build a firing range and a regulation trap and skeet range near the Exhibition Pasture at Craterville Park.

FBI agents, highway patrolmen, county sheriffs, and local police were always welcome to practice, free of charge and as much as they wanted. This was an opportunity for them to stay proficient and enjoy shooting as a sport. Indeed, it was generous to allow the officers to take advantage of the gun range. However, it was no coincidence that there was seldom a day or a special event when peace officers and their cars weren't visible around the park.

Dad supported police officers in another way. At that time, Oklahoma Highway Patrolmen usually rode one police officer to a car while on duty. Often, unreliable police radios were their only link to call for backup assistance, and in many cases, the next closest patrolman might be miles away. There had been instances where officers riding alone had been overpowered, injured, or killed on duty, simply because they didn't have a backup partner present. Dan Combs asked Dad for help to convince the state legislature to institute policy changes and provide funds for two-person patrols. Dad used all of his influence with his contacts and acquaintances to support the proposal. He also testified at hearings with state congressional committees in Oklahoma City. There were other people in addition to Dad who lobbied for changing the OHP policy, and soon there were two officer teams on patrol in many rural areas especially at night. Dad's help did not go unnoticed by OHP officers in southwest Oklahoma, and they often stopped by the park to thank him and shake his hand.

34. SPECIAL EVENTS

Running Craterville Park would be a full-time job for almost anyone. Even with Mom and Mamo both active in the business, it must have been a challenge. Between 1933 and 1957 Dad was between 18 to 44 years of age, and he was never satisfied doing just one thing. I'll cover a few of the highlights.

The Boy Scouts of America had asked for permission to build barracks where scouts to stay on summer camps. The land had been set aside from the Craterville Township. Dad donated the material, and the organization donated the construction labor. The location chosen was roughly a quarter of a mile northwest of the skating rink location and on the west side of Crater Creek. The project was a win-win deal for the park and the BSA. The barracks was a large wood-framed building with covered porches around the outside providing cooling breezes on summer nights. The building would sleep about 250 kids and scout leaders on bunk beds on the inside and the porches. The building was also used for summer camps planned by Dad, including band camps, football camps, and traditional summer activity camps. The Masonic Home for Boys and Girls also used the facility for summer outings.

The Scout House at Craterville Park.

Brochures advertising Craterville Park summer camps.

A 1949 full-page story in the Daily Oklahoman written by Special Correspondent Larry Grove gives a thorough account of the annual football camp. It says, in part, "almost 350 prep footballers live, sleep, and eat football during two-week training camp...five schools from Texas and four from Oklahoma have set up camp at the resort...they are Chickasha, with a roster of 66, Waurika with 33 squad men, Velma-Alma with 30, and Anadarko with 44. Hereford, Texas brought a squad of 38, Henrietta 26, Bowie 40, and Quitaque, Texas 27. Crowell, Texas uses the Craterville training field but is headquartered at nearby Medicine Park, brought 30. Dalton Criswell, head man from the Hereford Whitefaces quoted, 'The camp is an indispensable training aid. Where else,' Criswell questions, 'could I get all my boys to eat regularly, sleep regularly, stay out of mischief, and still get to practice on time?"

When Dad staged a promotion or camp, he believed hiring well-known individuals to judge, teach, direct, or be involved would lend credibility to the event. Such was certainly the case with the 1951 football camp at Craterville Park.

There were a pair of All-American football players who had just graduated from Oklahoma University in the spring. Both were natives of southwest Oklahoma and had recently become national football stars

177

while playing at OU. Darrell Royal and Bob Bodenhamer enjoyed success in their careers, especially Coach Royal, who would become one of the most famous college football coaches of all time while coaching at the University of Texas. Coach Bodenhamer would also gain prominence on a smaller stage while coaching state championship football teams at Lawton High School.

Hiring these two men and advertising them coaching the Summer Camp for Boys and the Football Training Camp produced a flood of applicants. About 350 boys attended each of the eight camp sessions scheduled in 1951 under their leadership. The boys were housed in the Scout House building, ate their meals at The Rush Inn, and had a full schedule of activities each day while utilizing the park amenities.

My personal recollection of Coach Royal's involvement would eventually become a cherished experience for me, but not for years to come.

I was five years old in 1951, but adventurous enough to want to spend the night with the "big boy" campers. Mom and Dad did allow me to spend the night in one of the park's cabins where Coach Royal and some other adults were staying. After midnight there was a big storm with plenty of thunder and lightning. I got scared and started crying and begged Coach Royal to take me home to our house across the park. He took me home where Mom calmed me down, which was more important to me that night than being brave like the big boys.

Flash forward to 2009. There was a performance at Bass Hall in Fort Worth, Texas depicting the life of the famous Texas panhandle rancher Charles Goodnight. Vickie and I attended, and by coincidence, Coach Royal was there. I introduced myself as Frank Rush, a name which he immediately recognized after some 58 years. He gave me a handshake, a big smile, and a warm hug. He immediately asked about Dad and Mom, both of which I was sorry to report, had passed away. He briefly related what a wonderful experience he, his wife Edith, and the Bodenhamers had at the park that summer years ago.

This is where my story comes to a classic Coach Royal conclusion. If you don't know, Coach Royal was widely renowned for his humorous and insightful quotes, and this is where I got my edition. I asked him if he remembered having to take me home in the middle of the stormy night because I was a scared five-year-old little boy. He laughed, then in his classic style replied, "No, I can't recall doing that, but don't be embarrassed, I had to take a lot of scared and crying college football players home while I was at UT!"

The stagecoach was driven by Coach Darrell Royal (standing and holding the reins) and Coach Bob Bodenhamer (seated and riding "shotgun"), posing for a picture with summer campers in 1951.

The annual Craterville Park Band Camp was the forerunner of band contests at both new Craterville Park and later in Texas at Sandy Lake Amusement Park. Again, the scout house, restaurant, and other park amenities made for a wonderful experience for the kids. Colonel Earl D. Irons was the nationally known Director of Bands at the University of Texas in Arlington, Texas, as well as a nationally recognized cornetist, composer, and clinician. He served as band camp judge and director and added a great deal of stature to the camps.

A uniformed high school band performing in front of the Indian Curio Store during one of the annual band camps at Craterville Park. c. 1956.

Yet another special event was billed as the Craterville Park Fly-In. A landing strip, just west of Highway 115 and the Craterville Park entrance sign, was cleared of rocks, mowed, and smoothed to accommodate the participants. A windsock and brightly colored flags marked the runway. A mention of the event in a newspaper article noted nearly two dozen airplanes were parked on the edge of the runway. While the novel event garnered attention as news stories, it lasted only a few years.

Chief Oscar Yellow Wolf greeted the pilots and their passengers as they arrived at the Annual Craterville Park Fly-In.

In keeping with the theme, cowboys greeted the pilots, their passengers, and guests, then delivered them by mule-drawn buckboards to their accommodations in the park cabins.

Dad never missed a chance to make a show out of a special event. When groups of adults had a meeting, retreat, or celebration Dad had a fire pit dug in the picnic grounds, and cooked "saddle blanket sirloin steaks" served with a pitchfork. The groups always loved the idea, and the steaks were always USDA Prime. The steaks were served on oversized ceramic platters with a baked potato, a roasted ear of corn, and a farmer's salad. The bill of fare would fill the stomach and imagination of the customers.

Dad cooked "Saddle Blanket Sirloins" and used a pitchfork to serve.

It looks like a pretty tasty dinner was served at the Craterville Park Fly-In.

The concept of Craterville Park as a tourist destination had been on the menu, so to speak since Granddad conceived the idea. Dad was at his best at presenting an appealing product when he advertised, and he always prided himself on delivering everything promised and more.

Spend Your Vacation
—at—

CRATERVILLE PARK-OKLA.

One of the Southwest's finest dude ranches, catering to people who enjoy clean, healthful recreation in beautiful surroundings.

DRIVE OUT TODAY

We have modern facilities for those who wish to spend a day, a week or a month in the Wichitas and especially appeal to those who seek a vacation for their families in proper surroundings.

Come on out and enjoy...

- Mountain Climbing
- Roller Skating
- Merry-Go-Round
- Cabins
- Horseback Riding
- Picnicking
- Minature Racers
- Zoo

RUSH INN provides good food at popular prices. Visit the meusom and curio shop for fine souvenirs. Our general store carries good stocks of supplies.

    Craterville Park was more than a special event site. Many people came there for a few hours to enjoy the natural beauty of the location, browse the Indian Curio store, laugh at the monkeys, or simply watch others having fun. Admission and parking were free!

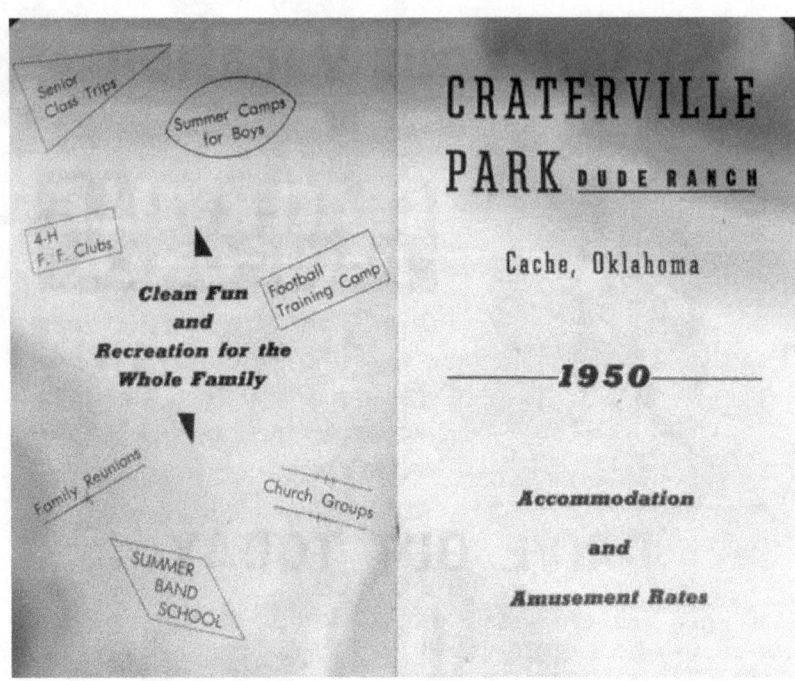

"Clean Fun and Recreation for the Whole Family" was what my grandparents and parents offered.

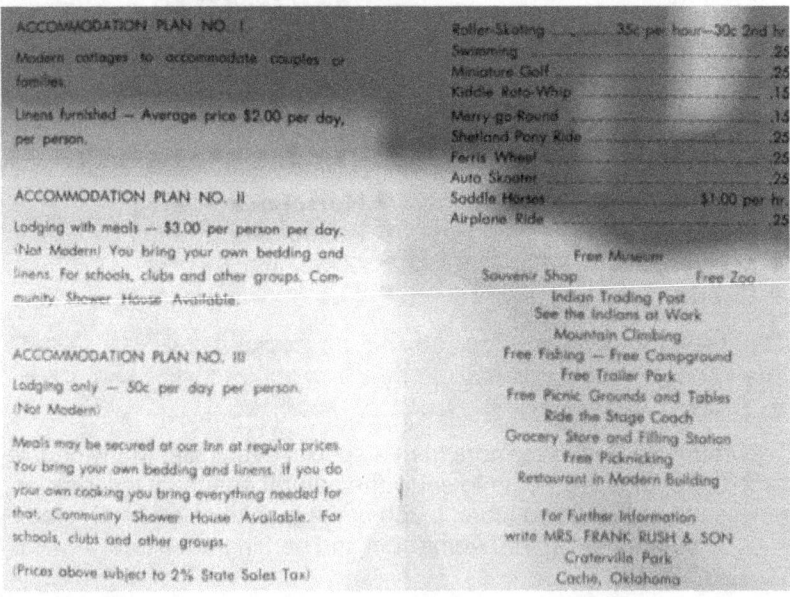

Compared to today, these prices look like a bargain.

An often-used publicity photo, and my all-time favorite, shows Dad in a red shirt (in the color edition), mounted on his favorite horse "Bill" and standing high atop a precipice above the Craterville Park swimming pool.

E. Frank Rush and Bill pose high above the swimming pool.

A brochure picture captures a group of boys enjoying a day of horseback riding, and touts Craterville Park as "The Heart of the Wichitas." I believe, for 34 years, Craterville Park was aptly portrayed.

What a way to make friends and memories.

35. THE ROCKING R RANCH

Craterville Park had a public side, but it was also the headquarters for Dad's more personal cattle and horse operations on the Rocking R Ranch. The eastern portion of the property containing 2505 acres of land, was prime ranch country.

The land in and around the Wichita Mountains is known for its quality and ability to range fatten cattle. Old timers stood by the conviction that a few mouths full of Comanche County grass would put more pounds on a cow than a bale of hay from any other part of the country. This wasn't totally bravado and pride. Beef cattle and horses do thrive in these hills. Domestic herds shared the bounty with a lengthy list of wildlife that flourish here, and all this was true on the Rocking R Ranch.

In 1943, Dad and Ted Warkentin of Lawton purchased about one hundred head of Hazlett-bred registered Hereford cattle, a popular bloodline of the time. Ted owned Southwestern Stationery and Supply in Lawton and aspired to be in the cattle business. I asked Dad how he and Ted got to be partners, and he told me, "Ted had the money, and I had the grass."

On January 4, 1945, Dad and Ted held the first of three Warkentin & Rush Production Sales. In attendance were honorary guests from the American Hereford Association and Oklahoma A&M (now Oklahoma State University). Frank Reeves of the *Fort Worth Star-Telegram*, Bobby Vincent of *The Ranchman* magazine, O. R. Peterson of *The Cattleman* magazine, and Jewett Fulkerson of the *Hereford Journal* reported the event in person.

All three sales were successful, and even though their business partnership eventually ended, their life-long friendship did not.

The cover page from the Warkentin and Rush Hereford sale.

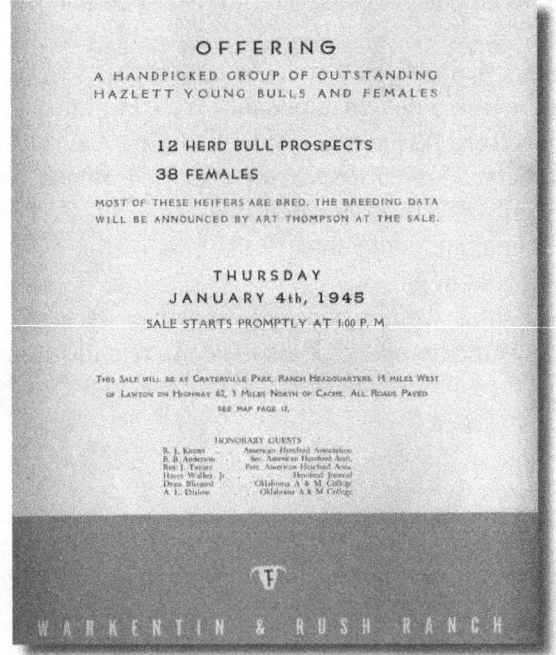

The introductory page from the Warkentin and Rush Hereford sale.

36. THE COW IN THE WELL

The story of the cow in the well started rather unceremoniously when one of Dad's cows fell into an unknown and abandoned well. The well was located near an old homestead on the east side of the ranchland. Dad missed the cow one day when he made his daily herd check. While searching for her, he ran across the caved-in well opening only to discover her looking up at him from the mud some twenty feet below. Some ranchers might have put the cow out of her misery and filled her grave at the same time. Dad, seeing an opportunity to save the cow and get a little publicity, called a wrecker and a photographer from the newspaper. As the photos show, the cow was successfully extracted. She gave birth to a healthy calf a few weeks later. Newspapers ran pictures and mentioned the cow belonged to the owner of Craterville Park.

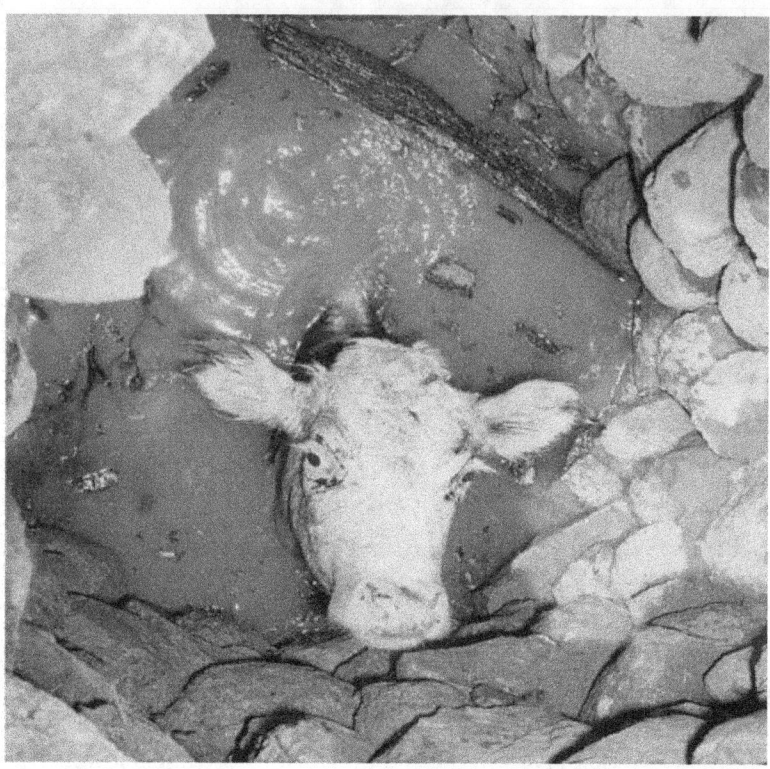

Curious people came to the park for years and asked about the cow in the well. Dad always had the cow (or a similar-looking cow) standing around the corrals to satisfy the curious public. These pictures were displayed in the Indian Curio Store and viewed with great curiosity.

37. PRETTY HORSES

Dad owned a great many saddle horses, Shetland ponies, and other personal horses he and Mom used on their frequent time in the saddle. Selective breeding organizations such as the Appaloosa Horse Club and the American Quarter Horse Association were forming in the late 1930s.

In the early 1950s, Dad began to purchase some registered Appaloosa mares. Dan Coates, Dad's friend from Fort Worth whom he had known since the rodeo days, owned a registered Appaloosa stud named Son of Quanah. Quanah certainly had one of the most popular bloodlines and eye-popping color to boot. Dad and Dan made a deal for Quanah to stay at the Rocking R Ranch and sire the colts for Dad's equally beautiful herd of forty to fifty Appaloosa mares. It was a good partnership, and Dad and Dan sold lots of colts from the herd that went on to show and perform on a high level in Appaloosa Association sanctioned shows.

Son of Quanah

In addition to being a great livestock range, there was plenty of good hunting and fishing on the Rocking R Ranch. Several lakes and farm ponds provided duck hunting and were brimming with game fish. Bobwhite quail flourished and Dad always kept a few good pointer birddogs. White-tailed deer were plentiful, and Dad invited friends to hunt and fish, sports that he and Mom relished all their lives.

In February 2024, Vickie and I visited what the military calls Lake Quanah today. It is in the heart of what was the Rocking R Ranch, and in my opinion, it is the quintessential lake of the Wichita Mountains.

Dad became a member of the Texas and Southwestern Cattle Raisers Association and registered his Rocking R brand. Registration with the TSCRA was a wise move on the part of any livestock owner because they had fieldmen who helped prevent livestock rustling. Their brand inspectors had the authority to arrest thieves, and they were good at their job. The location of the registered brand on an animal's body and the size of the brand was specified. Dad branded his cattle on the left hip with a five-inch brand and horses were branded on the right shoulder with a three-inch brand. Other ranchers could use the same brand but not in the same body position.

Dad's first Rocking R Ranch, fulfilled his dream of being a sportsman and rancher raising cattle and horses. Like the entertainment part of Craterville Park, the ranch was idyllic, profitable, and fun but the days were numbered until Craterville Park, and the first Rocking R Ranch would no longer be in Dad's possession.

38. PAPA JACK HOWENSTINE

Papa Jack Howenstine was a local legend, a neighbor, and a close friend of Dad's. Both men possessed an insatiable appetite to make a horse trade whether a horse was involved or not.

Papa Jack lived on his Oasis Ranch located on Highway 115 about one-half of a mile south of the entrance to Craterville Park. The ranch was a jumble of collectibles, tools, farm and ranch equipment, outbuildings, and assorted livestock. The inventory was kept in Papa Jack's head where he could recall each item and the amount of money he had paid or the trade deal he had made to acquire the object. He purchased cows by the pound and sold them by the head to ensure a deal would be made in his favor. In other situations, he might reverse the procedure to gain the upper hand. In either case, he almost always got the best end of a trade.

Papa Jack practically lived with a short cigar crunched between his teeth and had a sparkle in his eye that grew brighter when he was doing business.

While it was a great sport for the two of them to profit from a sale or swap between them, they would occasionally team up against a third party to make a trade.

Dad and Papa Jack were as close in their friendship as they were as neighbors. The Oasis Ranch and the Craterville Park horse pasture shared a common fence.

One day, a couple of men showed up at the Oasis Ranch driving a pickup and pulling a big horse trailer. They approached Papa Jack about purchasing some yearling colts. Papa Jack knew Dad had some colts for which he was asking $350 a head. By coincidence, the colts were in the park's adjoining pasture standing under some oak trees. They were visible but at a fair distance from where Papa Jack and the men were talking. Papa Jack pointed in the general direction of the colts and said he would "sell 'em for four hundred each, cash on the barrel head." Papa Jack correctly calculated Dad would gladly pay him a $50 commission for providing the buyers.

"Well, we were looking to buy some horses which cost a good deal more," one man said smugly. Papa Jack quickly solved the issue. He said, "My neighbor, Frank Rush, down the road at Craterville Park, has some purebred colts, and he'll take $800 rock bottom for 'em, only if he likes the looks of ya." Off went the men on their way to Craterville Park.

Papa Jack quickly called Dad and told him the men were on the way, and to not price the colts for a dime less than $800 each. Dad had the boys gather the colts from the horse pasture into the saddle horse barn while he was making small talk with the gents. The men looked over the selection, unaware they were the exact same colts Papa Jack had priced for $400 a short time earlier. They gladly paid cash at the premium price in one-hundred-dollar bills for five of the animals, loaded them in their trailer, and went happily on their way.

Papa Jack and Dad split the profit and the customers got exactly what they were looking for to boot. Papa Jack's eyes twinkled as always, as he crunched a fresh new stogie between his teeth.

This Papa Jack Howenstine drawing from Paul McClung's biography, *Papa Jack, Cowman from the Wichitas* captures the old cowman in a typical expression and his perpetual cigar. Permission was granted from Jerry and Paul McClung.

39. THE LAND GRAB

For 34 years Craterville Park flourished under Granddad and Dad's leadership, but what happened starting in early 1955 would have broken the spirit of a lesser man than E. Frank Rush. After much controversy and long bitter court battles, Craterville Park was condemned by the Army Corps of Engineers in Federal Court and taken into the Fort Sill military base. Needless to say, the Land Grab was devastating.

After the Korean War, the military was cutting back the number of operational bases. At the same time, long-range missiles with more firepower were advancing, and the Cold War had everyone nervous. Fort Sill was an important training facility for artillery, however, the cutbacks were a major threat to the base. The Army was looking for a larger firing range, possibly in Arizona.

As an aside to the Land Grab, history has a way of repeating itself. At least twice before Fort Sill's borders had been increased. The first incidence was the taking of land for the East Range which is generally east of what is now Interstate 44. Farms and ranches were purchased or condemned from their owners years earlier for that expansion. Next was the annexation of the Ketch Ranch which existed southeast of where the Wichita Mountains Visitors Center is now located. The cobblestone Ketch ranch house lies next to Highway 49 about a mile east of the center.

As the possibility of Fort Sill closing loomed, Lawton businesspeople realized Fort Sill could indeed close if steps weren't taken to bolster the importance and size of the facility. The land expansion for the base would play a key role in turning back the threat of closing the installation and crippling the local economy. For a time, the base's title was changed to Artillery and Missile Center to enlarge its scope and mission.

There were already rows of empty houses in Lawton, and rumors about moving the base to Arizona caused concern to snowball. They also thought the land to be condemned was of little value. The loss of Craterville Park, Comanche Chief Quanah Parker's historical home, and the other ranches involved was of little consequence to businessmen and the political establishment in Lawton, so they wholeheartedly endorsed the idea.

The Land Grab, as it became known, would soon be cited as the

195

most divisive issue in Southwest Oklahoma. Communities, neighbors, churches, and families were often deeply divided as a result of the controversy, and each side debated their views forcefully.

An op-ed story in the *Daily Oklahoman*, January 18, 1957, by RGM titled "The Smoking Room" defined much public opinion. The story stated, "Frank Rush does not know RGM is writing this piece. We haven't seen him in more than a year. And we're not concerned with the controversy that has been going on for two or three years among the leaders and spokesmen for wildlife, the war department, private enterprise, and commercial interest. We simply wish to say that Oklahoma needs more amusement centers like Craterville has been and, we hope, still will be.

In late 1955, Dad, rancher Wayne Rowe, and a delegation of landowners flew to Washington, D.C. to meet with the House Armed Services Committee. The government officials listened politely but had no intention of changing the proposal. The group returned home totally defeated.

Politicians, especially the 6th District Congressman, Victor Wickersham, publicly supported the landowners and stated that was no reason to take away the private land. Speaking with "two tongues," as our Indian friends say, he absolutely did not want to have an economic generator like Fort Sill lost during his term in office, regardless of who was hurt. When meeting with the supporters of the base expansion, he sided with them.

Fear was an ally for those who didn't have land involved in the deal. It was easy to argue that the land was needed for the defense of the nation.

The Right of Eminent Domain made it easier for the government to take private land back then. The Army Corps of Engineers was the government department dealing with the landowners, and the Corps used every tactic to accomplish its goal. The first thing anyone knew, the Corps persuaded one or two landowners in the western end of the proposed expansion to make a deal and sell out. Therein lies one part of their strategy. The Corps said some land had already been purchased, therefore, the land in the middle must be condemned to connect newly acquired land to the base.

Next, the Corps said the land they had already purchased, set the market price for the other land. While those few farmers who sold out early were pleased with their price, there was no comparison in actual land values. Also, the Corps did not want to pay extra for improvements or loss of business, such as Craterville Park. The land was just land to them, and the fact that Dad's property would be expensive, if not impossible to replace at any price, did not concern them.

Dad was served with papers that ordered him to allow appraisers to come to inspect and place a value on the property. The process moved along. Some landowners settled and some were heading for court, but one thing was certain, Craterville Park was going away.

Heartbroken and angry, Dad and some other owners hired lawyers and brought suits to Federal Court to fight the action. Congressman Wickersham sold out and did not stand up for the landowners as he had said he would. He supported the Land Grab, and many other congressmen followed his lead since the land was in Wickersham's district. As always, "you vote for my deal and I'll vote for yours," was how bills get passed in Congress. Dad's lawyer, Curtis Harris, took his fee, did a weak job of preparing the plaintiff's case, and was defeated by the powerful government lawyers in Federal Court in Tulsa. Dad recalled how Mister Harris turned to him and said, "Frank, you better take what they offer because that's all your old park is worth, and I can't help you anymore."

The Federal Judge made a finding in favor of the Corps' appraisers for $467,000 which was considerably lower than Dad's appraisers. The price averaged $186.00 per acre, however, the loss of business or moving expense was completely ignored.

The judge did leave a scrap of hope on the table, "to be mitigated later." The judge ruled that if the expenses of relocating the park exceeded the amount paid, Dad could present a claim to the government for the amount not to exceed $200,000. The expenses for moving verifiably exceeded that amount and two years later Dad submitted a claim. When the government reneged and refused to pay, Dad hired an attorney and sued for settlement in Federal Court. The trial took place in Tulsa, Oklahoma, in the fall of 1959. This time the Federal judge ruled in Dad's favor and awarded him the full $200,000. Any celebration was short-lived, however. The government's lawyers told Dad there were no funds appropriated to pay such a claim, even though he was successful in court. Dad's lawyer told him sewing the government for payment was risky, expensive, and would take years to settle so Dad did not pursue the case further.

Swallowing the bitter pill of the Land Grab was a devastating blow to Dad, but getting stomped on when he was down was unimaginable.

I have always equated this iniquity to how the Indian tribesmen surely felt when the US government defaulted on so many promises.

Herein lies the beginning of a problem that in a few short years would bring Dad to his knees, as you will see.

Two things never came to pass. First, the government claimed the property would be a dangerous place after the bombing practice began. Also, the highway from Cache to the south gate of the refuge would have to be closed to public traffic because it would be too dangerous for cars to travel through military property. The Corps of Engineers claimed the land would be like a war zone. Unexploded shells, land mines, and live fire training for soldiers would make the land extremely hazardous to anyone who might trespass. The picture they painted in the communities' minds was devised to persuade landowners their property was vital to the security of the country and would be used for that purpose only. In addition, no one can prove the security of the United States of America would be any worse if the Land Grab had been defeated.

In the early fall of 1977, when Vickie and I were visiting friends in Cache, we decided to take our kids, David and Jodi, through the refuge. At about noon, we headed north along Highway 115. When we got to the Craterville Park entrance, an army sign read "Camp Eagle," where the Craterville Park entrance sign had once stood. The gate was open, and signs were warning against trespassing on government property. Oddly enough, a paper sign was taped to a post announcing "Officers Fall Picnic" with an arrow pointing down the old entrance road.

I drove in and figured the worst they could do was toss me in the guardhouse, tow our car, and put the kids and Vickie in some kind of protective custody. Down the road we went, and to our surprise, there were about five hundred soldiers in uniform and their families standing around tables with white tablecloths and a big catering truck. The setting was near where our homes once stood, and the amusement park site was neatly maintained. The old store building, the restaurant, and our family house still stood in place. Signs on the store building doors directed military personnel to the offices used to manage recreational activities. To the east, where the Rocking R Ranch once existed, military families fished and picnicked at the lake with the big cement dam (Quanah Lake). I learned later that Camp Eagle (the Craterville Park property) was often used for army social events, military hunters, and fishermen who found those sports at their disposal, which is still the case today. The army even allowed the (Quanah) Parker Family

Reunion to hold its annual celebration on the site for several years.

I never found the courage to tell Dad or Mom about our visit to Camp Eagle. There was no need to break their hearts again. Dad, and our family, never fully recovered from the pain and inequity of losing our home, but the Lord gave us the strength to move on. Looking back, the realization the Rush family was just a brief steward of that special place, gave us some closure and a close bond to the ancient Indian families who once lived among those red granite rocks.

Southwest Oklahoma lost what would probably remain today as the largest and most entertaining tourist destination in that part of the state. A family-run business, led by two of the most energetic men in the amusement business, might still be a part of the culture and diversity of the community.

In the fall of 1956, Craterville Park was stripped of improvements and abandoned as ordered. The playground, home, and workplace for a community faded into history.

The Craterville Park equipment was moved to new Craterville Park. Our family moved to the new Rocking R Ranch north of Meers. The Rocking R Ranch Rodeos and the Indian Curion Store were moved to Cache. That time was certainly a milepost for us. It was a turning point for Mom and Dad who lived a long and interesting life together.

Vickie and I would probably have never met. We would not have wound up with a successful business at Sandy Lake Amusement Park for 48 years. The prospect of not having Vickie in my life and having our children and grandchildren helps me accept the Land Grab as our destiny.

I pray the Comanche and the Kiowa people feel the same.

40. NEW CRATERVILLE PARK

During the late 50s and early 60s, the next generation of people enjoyed new Craterville Park. Nestled in the western extremities of the Wichita Mountains, the new park would, once again, entertain and foster golden memories for families.

The question of where to relocate the park, and how the Quartz Mountain location was chosen, goes back to Mom's family history. Mom was born and raised in Blair, Oklahoma near the west end of the Wichita Mountain range. As discussed in an earlier chapter, Mom and Dad met and married at Craterville Park in 1933, and they often visited her family and home in Blair. They also visited nearby Quartz Mountain State Park after it was opened in 1937. Their attention was renewed when Quartz Mountian State Park Lodge was opened in 1955. The area had some characteristics resembling Craterville Park, primarily the Wichita Mountains.

In 1956, when Dad realized he was really going to lose Craterville Park, more than one site was considered for relocation. However, his familiarity with Quartz Mountain and Mom's family history in Blair, and a leap of faith helped finalize the decision. Dad, Uncle Royce Walker, along with Dad's foreman Bob Kirk road-sided the area and came up with the plan to build a new park on a piece of property near the entrance to the state park. The land had some sandy hills that could easily be leveled and developed. The scenic backdrop of the granite mountains clenched the deal in Dad's mind. The shape of the property was ideal for the placement of the various attractions to be installed. Water and electrical utilities were nearby, and the property had frontage for good exposure on a newly paved road. Dad was able to purchase the property at an attractive price because no one placed much value on the desert-like sand hills.

Dad didn't want to give up the market base of Craterville Park. He thought the new park would draw some customers from the old park even though the two properties were about fifty miles apart. Possibly the biggest asset of all was nearby Lake Lugert and the state park with hotel rooms, campgrounds, and boat docks that provided a readymade customer base.

There was another big advantage. Altus Air Force Base was just sixteen miles down the road on the east side of Altus. Dad had always cultivated the business Fort Sill military personnel provided at Craterville Park, and he realized the Air Force servicemen and their families would also make good customers.

Dad had lots of talents, but his ability to "ride herd" and make things happen in double quick time was one of his specialties. The move also reestablished his drive and determination. Such was the opening of new Craterville Park. Not to mention, he couldn't afford to let an operating season pass without income. Dad later recalled, "They took our land, but we moved everything that wasn't tied down and some things that were."

Starting in the fall of 1956, many attractions from Craterville Park were moved and reestablished within five months at new Craterville Park. The rides, equipment, inventory, several buildings, saddle horses, zoo animals, and the park's stellar reputation changed locations at an astonishing speed. With a sense of urgency and the help of friends, family, and loyal longtime employees new Craterville Park sprang out of the sand dunes in a bend of the North Fork of the Red River, by the spring of 1957.

A 1958 aerial photo of new Craterville Park. The racetrack/rodeo arena is in the foreground and the amusement area is in the upper left. Lake Lugert Dam is visible in the upper right corner.

As Craterville Park was dismantled, the necessary decisions were made to construct new Craterville Park. Uncle Royce was a dirt placement expert and took the task of bulldozing the sand hills and shaping and paving the property in preparation for the upcoming move.

Bob Kirk, Rusty Wahkinney, and other trusted employees quickly dismantled Craterville Park and then moved the buildings, rides, and equipment. Jesse and Red Robertson, the carpenters from Lawton who had helped Dad rebuild after the Indian Curio fire in 1955, were assigned the task of building various structures for the new park and getting the infrastructure for the rides in place. Laying out a park that would appeal to the eye, allowed for good traffic flow, and fitted the footprint of the new property, proceeded smoothly. In the capable hands of Uncle Royce, Bob, and Rusty, and with Dad orchestrating the operation, new Craterville Park burst to life.

A 1957 wide view of new Craterville Park looking northwest across Highway 44A and just south of the bridge leading to Quartz Mountain State Park.

A busy day with a parking lot full of cars at new Craterville Park.

New Craterville Park had most, but not all, of the same attractions as the old park. At the new park, the main building housed an office, a dark house walk-through maze, a glass house, a Pretzel ride, a skating rink, and a bumper car building. It had similarities to the main building at the old park. All the buildings had log and pine exteriors created by milled half-round lumber, a style that gave the buildings a rustic yet appealing appearance.

The main building at new Craterville Park contained the park office, glass maze, dark maze, Pretzel Ride, skating rink, bumper cars (Skooter), and an arcade.

At new Craterville Park, the Carousel Building is in the foreground, the Fly-O-Plane ride to the right, and the train station, kid ride building, and Rock-O-Plane to the left. The Lodge at Lake Lugert was located just beyond the granite mountain.

The new refreshment stand was conveniently located in the center of the rides and attractions. By the second season, an Indian Curio store was added to the front of this structure.

A busy day in the Kid Ride building. c. 1958

By coincidence, Joan and Lynn Foster from nearby Granite, Oklahoma worked at new Craterville Park. Little did I know, at the time, they had a younger sister, Vickie Foster, who would eventually become my sweetheart, wife, and life partner.

The rides and train station were clustered in the middle of the property. The track for the miniature train made a big loop toward the back of the property. Inside the loop was the park stage, similar to the old park. There was a monkey pen, a snake pit, and a big picnic pavilion constructed on the southern side of the complex. During the first year of operation facilities for the saddle horses were located near a big sand hill and pasture at the southwest corner of the property.

In the middle of the complex was a combination Indian Curio

Store, a refreshment stand, and an awning to cover the kiddie rides. The Fly-O-Plane, Rock-O-Plane, Tilt-A-Whirl, and the train station completed the midway.

A maintenance building stood behind the office building on the north side of the property with a cook shack nearby where employee's meals were prepared and served.

The Fly-O-Plane ride.

The Rock-O-Plane ride.

The American Flyer train driven by Frank Rush III in this picture served until it was replaced by the new C.P. Huntington train in 1959.

Jimbo, Shetland pony rides, and saddle horses were popular attractions at new Craterville Park, much the same as Craterville Park.

Like Craterville Park there was never a supply shortage of rattlesnakes from the nearby Wichita Mountains.

Overall, there was no mistaking the new for the old locations, but the similarities outweighed the differences. There was no swimming pool, public restaurant, or grocery store, but Dad added some attractions at new Craterville Park. A four-stall carnival game added color to the midway, even though Dad never liked the idea of having the park look too much like a carnival. Also, the saddle horse rentals were replaced by the racetrack after one year of operation. The saddle horse rental attraction never really took off, and it was getting difficult to find gentle horses. In addition, liability was starting to be a concern.

The huge sand hill on the south edge of the property didn't have much use except as a saddle horse riding area. Dad began to look for another attraction to put in the space.

Lanny Edwards was a race car driver and promoter at a dirt track speedway in Lawton. Another man, Clinton Herring, owned an automobile dealership in Lawton, and he and Dad had promoted some stunt car shows together. Lanny and Clinton convinced Dad that a quarter-mile dirt track would be a sure thing for weekly races at the park. Dad liked the idea, but there were issues with the necessary space for such an attraction. The fact was any race car driven over the sloped embankment of a normal track would run into the nearby amusement rides and other attractions. Lanny, Clinton, Uncle Royce, and Dad met in the fall of the first season at new Craterville Park to find a solution.

Lanny had traveled across the country racing cars, and he explained to Dad there were paved racetracks with retaining walls for the race cars. The idea of a paved track was out of the question, and dirt track racing was much more popular with local racers. The group did a little brainstorming and came up with the novel idea of enclosing a dirt track with a wooden retaining wall. Telephone poles buried deep and close together with heavy 4 x 12-inch wooden timbers lining the poles would serve as a more than adequate barrier. Lanny or Clinton couldn't recall a similar track anywhere. Dad asked, "Well, will it work?" The reply was, "Well, yeah, we believe so." Dad asked if a rodeo arena could be placed on the infield of the track so the facility would have dual use. Again, they remarked, "Well, sure we can." Dad's reply to the group was, "Men, let's get started."

Uncle Royce was given the task of reshaping the sandy hill and pouring concrete bleachers on the front side of the slope facing the track. In front of the grandstand, red clay for the track was brought in to provide an ideal surface for the car races. As planned, a set of rodeo bucking and roping chutes were erected on the infield of the track. The grandstand could seat about 3,000 people so Dad began dreaming about crowds pouring into the park for all the action.

The newly built racetrack, grandstands, and retaining wall are shown while under construction in the spring of 1958.

Occasionally, Dad would schedule a rodeo rather than races. The rodeo livestock would be trucked over from the ranch at Meers. Riding clubs from Altus, Duke, and Hobart were invited to sponsor the rodeos. With the riding club members selling advance tickets, their club got a portion of the sales price, and the rodeos did a booming business.

There were some auto thrill shows touring the country during the early 1960s including Johnny King's Daredevils and Thrill Circus, Joie Chitwood Thrill Show, and Midget (car) Auto Racing. Clinton Herring was acquainted with the promoters who booked the tour dates, and Dad had the new Craterville Park racetrack. All three special shows played to a full grandstand and put the new Craterville Park Raceway in the limelight.

Lanny Edwards organized the stock car races, collected the entry fees, and paid the winners. There were usually one or two entries from every town for miles around. Local mechanics or a small group of "good ole boys" would patch up an old junk car, hand paint a number on the door, and haul it to the races. To increase horsepower mufflers were replaced by straight tailpipes. For safety, it was required that the drivers had to remove the gas tanks and use a container holding only one gallon of fuel, which was just enough to run the race. Other than that, car owners didn't have much invested. Since there wasn't much to lose, the races were crazy and wild.

Crashes were frequent on the track and fist fights in the race pit between rival drivers occurred almost as often. Lanny Edwards, wielding a tire iron, tried to keep order, but the slugfests in the race pit area were occasionally the most exciting part of the event.

The sound of the race announcer's voice amplified by loudspeakers, and the thundering tailpipes echoing off the wall around the track were deafening. Dad usually announced the races himself, but occasionally he let me call the action. It was an easy task. All you had to do was announce the number of the car and the name and hometown of each driver as the cars made their warmup laps. More importantly, the announcer had to sound excited as the race progressed and wrecks happened. During the race, the car noise overpowered the PA system to the point the announcer's words were inaudible, but Dad instructed me to, "Just keep yelling into the microphone no matter what." Once I screamed, "The driver of car twenty had scrambled eggs, bacon, and toast for breakfast this morning!" The crowd didn't understand a word I said, but they went wild anyway!

The racetrack vision came true. The racetrack attracted big crowds almost every weekend. The events were usually held on Friday and Saturday nights. The live performances on the park stage were usually on Saturday and Sunday afternoons. Some weekends both venues were booked, and of course, there was always a free fireworks show on the Fourth of July.

The racetrack with a crowd and some early model cars was loud and exciting. The park's attractions lay just beyond the outer wall.

The race car drivers were a tough bunch, but the wall was tougher. Drivers did not have anything like modern protection. Most drivers tied themselves to the seat with a piece of rope and wore football helmets for some limited shielding. Johnson Funeral Home had their ambulance on site just in case.

This is a newspaper ad for one of the thrill shows at the Craterville Park Speedway.

A high school band performs on the infield at new Craterville Park Speedway. The rodeo bucking chutes are seen in the background.

Dad knew, if free shows would draw the crowds, the rides and other attractions would pay the bills. There was a charge for the amusement rides, the racetrack events, and the rodeos, but the stage acts were always free.

Like the former park, new Craterville Park had a show stage, with lights and a sound system. Because there wasn't a grass lawn in front of the stage, like the old park, bleachers were added for overflow crowds.

The performance stage at new Craterville Park.

Benny and Betty Fox billed themselves as the Sky Dancers. The couple performed on a fourteen-inch diameter dance floor high atop an eighty-foot pole. They danced in many styles from ballroom to waltz, to boogie-woogie, and everything in between. Please note the platform was fourteen inches, not fourteen feet. The act featured prerecorded music that bounced from one familiar song style to another as the Sky Dancers changed dance steps and costumes in mid-air. Benny wore a white tuxedo, and Betty had a dress that could be quickly rearranged to match the dance style. It was a very novel act, not to mention the fact that there were eighty feet of thin air between the edge of the dance floor and solid ground.

Benny and Betty Fox, "The Sky Dancers."

The Sky Dancers played at both Craterville Park and new Craterville Park. Dad staged a publicity stunt for the duo in downtown Altus, Oklahoma, the largest town near new Craterville Park. The tallest building in Altus was only six stories tall, but still an imposing height for the exciting exhibition. Mister Fox had a specially designed dance platform, which could be suspended out eight feet beyond the edge of a rooftop. The dance floor disc and supporting steel structure, along with dozens of sandbags for counterbalance, had to be lugged up six stories of the structure. A crew of new Craterville Park employees labored for hours to put the prop on the roof. At noon on Friday, July 2, the Fox team entertained surprised businesspeople around the town square with a sample routine called "Dancing on the Clouds." Publicity notices were scattered to the wind from atop the building. "Bring the family, friends, and neighbors to Craterville Park July 3rd and 4th, and see the full show," announced the notices. The newspaper ran a picture, and the largest crowds to attend a novelty act at new Craterville Park were on hand that Saturday and Sunday.

Some of the stars and acts at the new park had also appeared in earlier years at Craterville Park, but time and popularity had evolved as new personalities rose to prominence. Comedian Minnie Pearl, actor Dale Robertson from *The Tales of Wells Fargo,* and western music singer and TV star Rex Allen performed at both parks. The newer stars who made appearances at new Craterville Park included Clint Walker from the TV series *Cheyenne*, Robert Horton the handsome star of *Wagon Train,* and Donna Douglas, a.k.a Elly May Clampett of *The Beverly Hillbillies*. On several occasions, the Rocking R Ranch Rodeos were held at Cache on the same day as events at new Craterville Park. Some stars appeared at Cache shortly after noon and then were driven to new Craterville Park for a later appearance.

When Robert Horton came to the park, there were a lot of kids, but the main part of the crowd was young girls and women. Horton had several hit songs including "They Call the Wind Mariah," and he acted in the musical *Oklahoma,* and other stage and screen appearances. He was best known for playing Flint McCullough on the number-one television show, *Wagon Train*. He was so handsome the ladies screamed and tried to get close enough to touch him. The crowd nearly got out of hand, but the park employees kept him secure enough to sign autographs without having his shirt torn off. There were several state troopers in Oklahoma Highway Patrol cars at the park to help direct traffic and keep things orderly. Dad asked one of the troopers to pull his squad car near the platform where Horton signed autographs. After it was long past the time for Horton's scheduled departure, he was safely hurried into the back seat of the OHP cruiser. With lights flashing and siren wailing, he left the park for the airport. The crowd was euphoric, and boy Dad was happy!

Clint Walker played Cheyenne Brody on the TV series *Cheyenne*.

Robert Horton played Flint McCullough on the TV series *Wagon Train*.

Michael Landon played Little Joe Cartwright on *Bonanza*.

Singer Molly Bee had several hits including. "I Saw Momma Kissing Santa Claus."

Henry Haynes and Kenneth Burns, better known as Homer and Jethro, were a comedy/musical duo. They performed at the height of their popularity when their parody rendition of "How Much is That Hound Dog in the Window" was released. The crowd cheered until they sang the song for the third time in two encores.

Homer and Jethro.

The Grand Ole Opry stars always drew big crowds. They usually accompanied themselves on the guitar, but sometimes they were accompanied by a two or three-piece band. Little Jimmy Dickens and Brenda Lee sang for over an hour on stage in the hot sun, then autographed pictures until everyone had a copy.

Rex Allen was known for his unique voice, his western style ballads, movie and television roles, and as a film narrator.

A huge crowd seeking a free autographed souvenir photo from Robert Horton star of *Wagon Train* at new Craterville Park.

By the mid-1960s, Dad started hiring professional wrestling stars. He had a wrestling ring built on top of the show stage complete with a semi-flexible floor and rope fences. Dan Coates, Dad's Appaloosa horse partner, was also a famous rodeo and wrestling announcer from Fort Worth. Dan helped Dad start booking the wrestling shows, and he was also hired to announce the matches.

Danny "The Bull Dog" Plechas was not only the popular bad guy, but he was also one of the main promoters for the other wrestlers. Dan would caution the crowd, "Please don't bark at The Bull Dog," which would always bring howls and yaps from the audience. Plechas would hold his ears and run around the stage in obvious agony, which always incited the crowd to bark louder.

The wrestlers traveled on a regular weekly circuit. They wrestled in Shreveport, Louisiana, on Friday night and at the Sportatorium in Dallas on Saturday. On Sunday afternoon, they would stop by the park for a match on their way to Amarillo for a Sunday evening show. The weekly tour brought them back to North Side Coliseum in Fort Worth for the televised "Monday Night Wrestling" show.

At the park, wrestling shows were held at 2 p.m. on the open-air stage, and it was often sweltering, a condition to which the wrestlers and fans paid little attention. There were the usual bad-guy/good-guy matches, and even women and midget wrestlers made special appearances. The audience would take sides and return the next weekend to see a promised rematch or grudge match featuring their hero. The wrestling grew wilder and more popular each week.

One unusual thing, which few people realized, was the four wrestlers and the referee usually traveled together in the same car. This was a "wrestling demonstration" for the pros, but it was the real deal in the eyes of the customers. When the five-man crew would arrive, Dad would hide them in one of the houses at the park where they dressed and prepared for the match. He would have one of his employees load two wrestlers in a hidden car and bring them to the stage from a different direction, so spectators didn't realize they had arrived together. The mayhem and chaos started in earnest when all four wrestlers got on the stage.

Pro wrestling is like a soap opera, gym meet, dinner with your in-laws, and a cockfight all rolled into one. If you asked a pro wrestler if it's all an act, they would likely invite you into the ring to find out first-hand. People should never accept that challenge.

Rock and Roll was all the rage in the late 50s and early 60s, so what better place to hold a sock hop than the skating rink? It was a fantastic idea since the infrastructure was already in place. Admissions could be controlled at the door. The skating rink concession stand with the adjoining arcade and bumper cars would create additional revenue. A coin-operated jukebox was hooked up to loudspeakers. The sock hops were scheduled only a handful of times each season on Saturday nights at very conservative hours from 7 to 10 p.m. School-age teenagers paid admission, and each was required to be accompanied by a parent. Parents made the best chaperones and were admitted free if they promised not to dance. Overall, it was a safe and fun place to do a little "twisting" on the skate floor.

New Craterville Park catered to the enlisted men and their families at Altus Air Force Base just as Craterville Park had done with Fort Sill personnel. Both bases would haul busloads of enlisted men to the parks, and they were good customers. Dad would call on the base commanders, and they were always enthused about sending troops to a location where there was scarce probability of trouble.

The local newspapers and the radio stations in Altus and Hobart were glad to sell Dad some airtime and, in addition, run a news story on the events at the park. Dad had more than a few skills but getting in the news was perhaps his favorite challenge.

During the years at new Craterville Park families visited the park and took "golden memories" home with them. The younger generation who remembered only new Craterville Park had the same fondness people had for the old park.

41. ROCKING R RANCH RODEOS

Recalling the Land Grab, the improvements at Craterville Park still belonged to Dad so naturally he moved them and put them back to work. While building new Craterville Park, Dad decided to move the recently reconstructed Indian Curio Store, Jimbo the giant steer, the live rattlesnake exhibit, and a refreshment stand to Cache. In addition, his itch to get back in the rodeo business was flaring up and the Cache location fit the bill. He figured the Indian Curio Store would have a good customer base of people visiting the Wildlife Refuge. Jimbo was certainly a traffic stopper, and a rattlesnake pit was easy to recreate. The handful of attractions fit the location and Cache was a source for great employees, as it had always been.

The Cache location was just three miles south of Craterville Park and at the southwest corner of the old Highway 62 and Highway 115. Be reminded that old Highway 62 is now called Cache Road NE and passes through Cache on its southern border. The new Highway 62 now passes on the north side of Cache and did not exist at the time.

The new Indian Curio Store had replaced the store and museum building destroyed by fire only a couple of years earlier. The new building was too good to leave behind, but too large to move in one piece. Jesse and Red Robertson came up with a plan to literally cut the building into two pieces so that moving trucks could haul each half separately. The plan worked, and the building was put back together at the new location in Cache.

In 1960, Dad installed a train track around the Cache property and purchased his first C.P. Huntington #8 miniature train from Chance Mfg. in Wichita, Kansas. There wasn't enough foot traffic at Cache to make the Chance train profitable. At the same time, the American Flyer train which had been moved from Craterville Park to new Craterville Park needed replacing. Thus, Dad sold the American Flyer train and moved the newer Chance train from Cache to new Craterville Park to open the 1962 season.

Dad's newly revived Rocking R Ranch Rodeo Company began holding weekly rodeos at Cache, and he purchased a string of rodeo stock from Bill Yale, a Texas rodeo producer. The following year Dad purchased 10 additional bucking bulls from Tommy Steiner, a famous rodeo producer from Austin, Texas. That was enough stock to produce rodeos at nearby towns on Thursday, Friday, and Saturday nights from March to October and return to Cache for Sunday matinées.

Quite a few nearby towns held summer rodeos. When the local rodeo committees noticed how successful the Rocking R Ranch rodeos were, they started asking Dad to produce the shows in their hometowns. The circuit included the towns of Apache, Chattanooga, Walters, Fairview, Rush Springs, Mountain View, Carnegie, Hollis, Walters, Waurika, Guthrie, and Anadarko, all in Oklahoma. The Altus, Hobart, and Duke, Oklahoma rodeo committees sponsored rodeos at new Craterville Park. Those three rodeos were staged on the infield of the racetrack at the park. Rocking R Ranch rodeos in Texas included Burkburnett and Bowie. On Labor Day, July 4th and Memorial Day we stayed home and had three-day rodeos at the arena in Cache.

Although these were not professional rodeos sanctioned by the Rodeo Cowboys Association, Dad's production, skilled contestants, and outstanding livestock were highly praised by customers. Dad offered his expertise in marketing to the rodeo committees in advance of each event, which usually resulted in capacity crowds.

There were lots of great cowboys entering each week, one of which was Junior Garrison from Marlow, Oklahoma who went on to win two RCA World Champion Calf Roping titles in 1966 and 1970. Regular contestants also included several bulldoggers from Burkburnett, Texas, including the 1964 RCA World Champion Bulldogger, C.R. Boucher. Each event had other heroes as well. There were skilled bull riders and bareback bronc riders aplenty, and the timed events of calf roping, bulldogging, and ladies' barrel racing were filled with talented contestants.

Paul McClung wrote a feature news article and ran a picture in the Lawton Constitution featuring Joe Louis, Dad's prized bucking bull. Joe Louis was a gentle pet while at home on the Rocking R Ranch, but he took on a different personality in the rodeo arena.

Joe Louis became famous in his own right. While Dad owned him, Joe was successfully ridden only one time. Dink Wicker, a young cowboy from Blair, Oklahoma stayed aboard the full eight-second ride at a rodeo sponsored by the Altus Round-Up Club Rodeo at the new Craterville Park arena.

Joe Louis enjoys a snack in one of his calmer moments. Photo courtesy of the Lawton Constitution.

The championship buckles presentation for the top annual money winners at Rocking R Ranch rodeos in 1965. From left: Frank Rush III, announcer and pickup man; Pepper Morgan, calf roping champion; Bill Abbott, bareback riding champion; Ken Williams, bull riding champion; Suzy Self, rodeo secretary; Gene Snider, rodeo judge; Nelda Patton, champion barrel racer; Donnie Bowles, champion bulldogger; Wild Willie Windsor, rodeo clown, and Tom Self, arena boss. The two cowboys standing on the chutes are unidentified.

Some stars and celebrities made personal appearances at the Cache Rodeos on the same day they performed at new Craterville Park. When possible, they would perform in the early afternoon during the rodeo at Cache and then be driven to new Craterville Park for a late afternoon show. TV stars such as Clint Walker from the series *Cheyenne*, Michael Landon a.k.a. Little Joe from *Bonanza*, Robert Horton from *Wagon Train,* and Donna Douglas starring as Elly Mae Clampett of *The Beverly Hillbillies* were among the performers who appeared at both places on the same day.

Donna Douglas, a.k.a. Elly Mae was really into the rodeo. She arrived at Cache about one hour before the show began and went around visiting with the cowboys and admiring their horses. When the rodeo began, she climbed up on the fence behind the calf roping chutes and enjoyed the rodeo as much as the fans. When it was time for her performance, all the cowboys gathered in the arena to watch.

Donna Douglas played Elly Mae Clampett on
The Beverly Hillbillies.

Dan Blocker, a.k.a Hoss Cartwright, was a fan favorite and drew a huge crowd at the Cache rodeo, however, his schedule did not allow time for him to appear at new Craterville Park. He was convincing enough in his TV role to be presented with a ceremonial Indian blanket from the Comanche Tribe at the end of his performance.

Dan Blocker played Hoss Cartwright on the #1-rated television show Bonanza from 1964 through 1967.

Hank Thompson, leader of the Brazos Valley Boys, was scheduled for two performances. Hank was well into his music career which lasted over five decades. His 1952 #1 hit song "The Wild Side of Life" and many of his 30 hit recordings were popular when he appeared at Cache. On his second visit, when Hank was supposed to appear, he didn't show up on time. The rodeo went on as scheduled, but when the show was over, due to Hank's absence, Dad announced that anyone who wanted a refund could get their money at the ticket office. The crowd cleared out about the time Hank showed up drunker than Hooter Brown. There was a dressing room for the stars nearby and Hank was inside waiting on Dad. He didn't have to wait long. Dad pushed Hank up against the wall, gave him a piece of his mind, and demanded his $500 deposit money back. Hank pulled out a big wad of one-hundred-dollar bills and peeled off five. That may have been the only time Dad failed to give a show as promised.

Hank Thompson
Country music star with over 30 top ten hits.

The incident with Hank was an exception. The production of the rodeos at Cache, especially when the stars made personal appearances, rivaled many of the bigger professional rodeos in the area. Once again, "golden memories" were the legacy of the Rocking R Ranch Rodeos.

42. THE BIG MATCH

Sixteen-time World Champion Cowboy Jim Shoulders and Dad were long-time friends. The same was true for bull riding legend Freckles Brown who had known Dad since the Craterville Park rodeo days. A brief history of the two men speaks for itself. Jim was the first cowboy to win 16 World Championship titles, and he was a Rodeo Hall of Fame inductee. Freckles was the first cowboy to ride Jim Shoulders' bull Tornado at the National Finals Rodeo in 1967. He was 47 years old at the time. He also was the World Champion Bull Rider in 1962 and a Rodeo Hall of Fame inductee in 1979.

In early 1965, Dad came up with the idea of having a matched bull riding between the two world champion bull riders at the Cache arena. Dad made a deal with Freckles and Jim to ride for a $300 winner-take-all purse. The match was advertised around Southwest Oklahoma, and on the day of the event, May 2, 1965, over three thousand people bought tickets to the event at the Rocking R Ranch Rodeo arena with seating for two thousand five hundred, however, no one complained.

In addition to the advertised match, an invitational jackpot bull riding for 25 bull riders was held. Jim and Freckles got to choose the invited bull riders. One young man chosen was a relatively unknown rough stock rider at the time named Larry Mahan. Jim predicted Larry would be a world champion. He was correct. Larry went on to win six All-Around Cowboy titles and two World Champion Bull Riding titles in professional rodeo.

Buck and Tommy LaGrand were contracted to be the clowns and bullfighters. The LaGrands were popular enough to attract their own crowd. The Lawton Rangers Rodeo Club Mounted Drill Team performed and added color to the show.

Both Jim and Freckles made qualified rides on each of the three bulls they drew, but Freckles prevailed by outscoring Jim.

The news coverage was even more extensive after the match than it was before. Rodeo contestants and rodeo enthusiasts alike hailed the event as historic. The event was successful, and all expectations were exceeded.

Another matched bull riding was quickly scheduled at Cache. The second match pitted Freckles Brown against Bill Kornell on June 6, 1965. Bill Kornell won the title of RCA World Champion Bull Rider in 1963. As a footnote to history, Freckles won both events.

The souvenir program from the first matched bull riding at the Rocking R Ranch Rodeo Arena in 1965.

A ticket from the second match bull riding between Freckles Brown and Bill Kornell, June 6, 1965.

Sixteen times World Champion Cowboy Jim Shoulders at Cache.

World Champion Bull Rider Freckles Brown
in front of the sellout crowd at Cache.

The Orbit section of the Daily Oklahoman newspaper featured the matched bull riding event in an article titled "Eight Second Fight." Frank Rush III holds the American flag and looks on as the grand entry serpentines through the arena during the opening ceremony.

The event was probably the first matched bull riding involving top contestants ever produced by anyone. At the National Finals Rodeo in December of 2004, I asked Jim Shoulders if it was the first time he remembered a matched bull riding being staged. He told me that there had been some rough stock buck-outs which included invited professional saddle bronc, bareback, and bull riders, but as far as he could recall it was the first time an event had been billed as a one-on-

one match. Jim said to me, "You know, I can't say Frank invented matched rodeo events, but the idea was new enough at the time that I would give Frank credit for putting those kinds of events in the minds of a lot of rodeo producers."

43. THE NEW ROCKING R RANCH

Dad was wheeling and dealing after losing Craterville Park. He was on life's amusement ride of his own design which seemed unceasing and dauntless, and our family strapped in for the ride with him,

Lucius Long owned a three thousand two hundred acre spread about fifteen miles north of Craterville Park near Meers. Mister Long let it be known the ranch was for sale. Dad asked a real estate man to negotiate a deal, and we soon had a place to move.

Dad and Mom rejoiced in naming our new home the Rocking R Ranch. They loved entertaining people, and the ranch was a personal way to enjoy their friends and raise cattle and horses.

There was a big two-story house, a horse barn, and another small house on the ranch. The property would have been beautiful without the mountains, but with the Wichita Mountain range serving as the backdrop, the view was magnificent. Mount Sheridan and Tarbone Mountain are possibly the most picturesque in the Wichita range and lie directly to the south. An unobstructed view of Mount Scott to the southeast completed the setting. The big game fence around the refuge joined the ranch on the south and west borders so there was plenty of privacy.

Medicine Creek wound through almost every pasture, and its deep pristine pools provided water year-round. The oak trees on the hills and pecan trees along the creek produced an abundance of acorns and pecans for wildlife.

Deer, fish, quail, turkey, dove, and elk made the ranch a paradise for any sportsman, or an eleven-year-old lad like me. There were bobcats, coyotes, critters of all kinds, and plenty of diamondback rattlesnakes to keep you alert. The native grasses provided rich nutrition for the Appaloosa horses, Quarter Horses, and Hereford cattle.

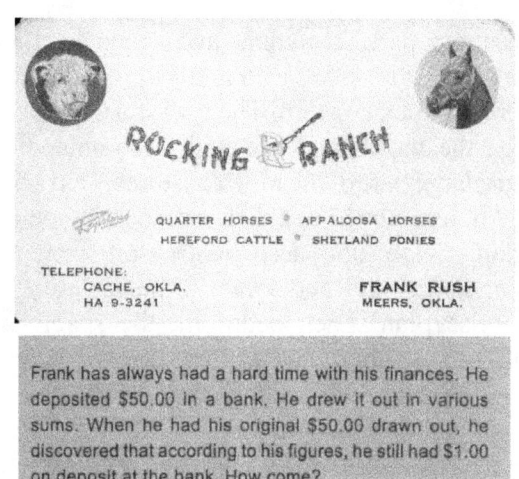

Dad's business card with a puzzle he enjoyed printed on the back.

The front entrance sign at the Rocking R Ranch.

The amusement park, ranching, and rodeo kept everyone busy. Adding to the activity in 1959, Dad and Mom decided to build a new house, but there was one concern. The two-story house on the property was located on the most ideal site with a commanding view of the mountains and a large part of the ranch pastures. Dad and Mom decided to have the old house moved to a different location on the property.

Once again, Jesse and Red Robertson were hired for the construction, and work got underway in the spring of 1960. It was a magnificent house plan. Each bedroom, the spacious living room, dining room, and kitchen shared the view looking toward the mountains. Large picture windows gave a pleasant view of the lawn, swimming pool, and the pastoral scenery beyond. The exterior of the new structure had the familiar log appearance. Flagstone porches and native rock appointments accented the style befitting the Wichita Mountains.

The living room included a fireplace large enough to burn logs four feet in length, and there were leather couches and several leather chairs arranged in the spacious room with a vaulted ceiling.

One humorous yet somewhat dangerous occurrence took place during construction. When excavation for the foundation work began, Jesse and Red ran into an underground rock. The men tried to dig it up, but it must have been the top of a buried mountain peak. They were stymied. If the rock could not be moved, the building would need to have plans changed considerably, so Jesse and Red came up with a dynamite idea. No kidding, we're talking TNT here. No one knew how much to use, but more seemed like a better choice than less, so a blast hole was dug under the rock and two sticks of explosive were loaded. The fuse was lit. Everyone ran about two hundred feet away and took shelter behind a wall, thinking we would be safe. Wrong! The explosion sounded like a howitzer at Fort Sill had gone off. About three seconds later, we peered out of our hiding place to see what happened. It looked perfect, and the rock in question was gone. Gone straight up in pieces, that is. It started raining rocks! Some were as big as grapefruit. Outside of damage to the barn roof and a few egos, no one was injured, and the construction of the house continued.

Dad and Mom in front of the ranch house
with the pastures and the beautiful
Wichita Mountains in the background.

The ranch house and pool at the Rocking R Ranch.

A view from the front porch looking toward Tarbone Mountain.

The living room was the site of frequent neighborhood parties.

A view of the ranch house in February 2024.

44. HOOFS AND HORNS

Dad bought some excellent quarter horses, mostly from Dr. W.C. Tisdal's Lazy T Ranch in Hallett, Oklahoma. Jimmy Tis was one of the registered Quarter Horse stallions Dad purchased. Jimmy Tis was used for breeding mares at the ranch and some outside customers' mares from other ranches. Jimmy Tis won several Oklahoma Quarter Horse Association shows and was recognized as the "Top Stallion of The Year" for Oklahoma at Pawhuska, Oklahoma in 1958. Dad purchased another stud from the Waggoner Ranch in Vernon, Texas, named Dun Star King, an own son of King P-234. Between those two studs and a herd of about eighty registered Quarter Horse mares, the Rocking R Ranch quickly gained notoriety.

The Appaloosa mares from Dad's partnership with Dan Coates at Craterville Park were moved to the ranch, and Son of Quanah was the principal sire for about thirty registered Appaloosa mares.

Dad maintained a herd of about one hundred registered horned Herefords cattle of Zato Heir and Hazlett breeding. This was the same bloodline which was successful at the first Rocking R Ranch. The registered cattle market in the late '50s and early '60s was very volatile, but Dad had been lucky enough to sell when the price was good or increase his herd size when the market was soft.

This herd of Quarter Horse mares was anxious to get back to grazing after leaving the corrals at the ranch.

Herding horses with a helicopter for a TV commercial filmed on the Rocking R Ranch. c.1960

The family at work gathers cattle on Tarbone Flat.

Dad started entering his best Quarter Horses in shows for family enjoyment, and in addition, to building a reputation for his herd. Jimmy Tis and Dun Star King were shown in the stallion classes. We showed four or five stud and filly colts that would later be used in his breeding program or sold in the annual sale. The Rocking R Ranch horses built a good reputation in the show ring.

Dad and Dan Coats of Fort Worth, the owner of herd sire Son of Quanah, continued to breed and sell registered Appaloosa horses at the ranch just as they had done at Craterville Park. Son of Quanah sired lots of colorful colts. These are two good examples.

Quanah's Warrior

Son of Quanah's Tomahawk

Dad started planning annual horse production sales in 1960. He would sell forty to fifty colts from his Appaloosa and Quarter Horse herds, eight or ten brood mares, some saddle horses, and usually two or three good stud colts we had proven in the show ring.

E. Paul Waggoner of the well-known Waggoner Ranch in Vernon, Texas, consigned ten yearling colts to the sales as well.

For the sales, a big tent with an auction ring was set up near the ranch corrals. There was a viewing of the sale animals the day before the event. Calf roping horses and other specially trained horses were exhibited the morning of the sale, and a barbecue meal was served to all who attended. The auctions were conducted by Colonel Walter Britten from College Station, Texas. Several hundred people attended.

After three successful annual auctions, Dad decided enough buyers were available for the annual colt crop to be sold at private treaty. After 1963, buyers would visit the ranch to purchase horses. Without the expense of the auction, the net gain was an advantage. For many years, you could see the Rocking R brand on horses at rodeos, horse shows, and anywhere else horsemen gathered, and they always represented their owners well.

The action of the auction in the sale arena with auctioneer Col. Walter Britton calling the sale. Dad is shown second from left.

The front and back cover of the 1960 sale catalog.

A 1961 horse sale advertisement.

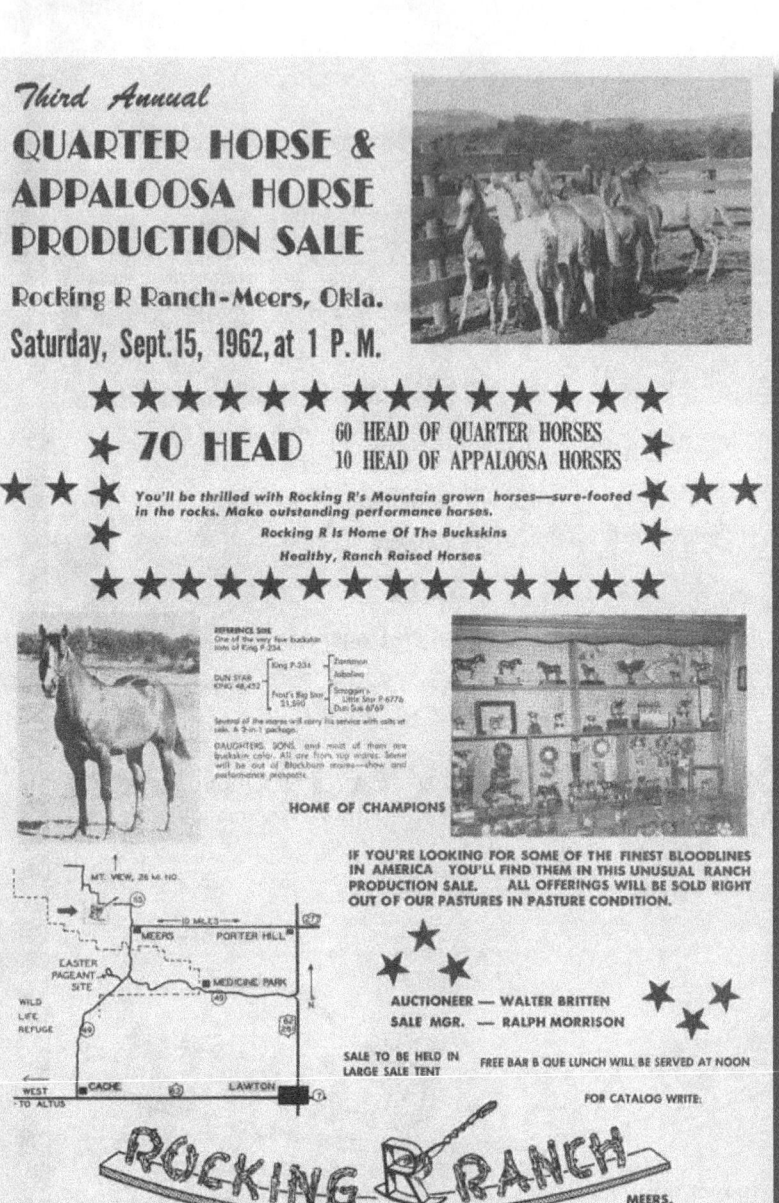

A 1962 advertisement flyer for a Rocking R Ranch sale.

45. A HOLLYWOOD VISIT

In 1957 and 1958, Walt Disney produced a television show titled *The Saga of Andy Burnett*. The show ran for several weeks as a serial, depicting the life of a pioneer who traveled from Pittsburgh to the Rocky Mountains.

A location scout came to the area in the early spring of 1958 and looked at the Wichita Mountains Wildlife Refuge and herds of buffalo. There were some problems with filming the action scenes. Panoramic scenes of the buffalo were acceptable in the refuge, however, the need for stunt work and depictions of Indians chasing the buffalo were out of the question. The movie scout came to the ranch to talk to Dad about leasing the ranch property where the buffalo hunt could be filmed. The scout liked the location with the mountains in the background. They agreed on the price, and a deal was made.

The film being shot did not contain dialog, so not all the star actors came to Oklahoma. Instead, the second unit film crew and stunt doubles, along with several film trucks filled with equipment, arrived to do the job. Actor Iron Eyes Cody portrayed the lead character Mad Dog, the film's Indian chief, but he did not come to the ranch. Iron Eyes Cody's stunt double was Buddy Heaton from Kansas. Buddy had a well-deserved reputation as a wild and rowdy character. Yakima Canutt was the second unit director. Canutt was famous in Hollywood for his portrayals of cowboys in Western movies, and he was a former World Champion Saddle Bronc rider and a seasoned actor. Notably, Canutt had been the second unit director of John Ford's movie *Stagecoach*. Canutt also staged the chariot races for the movie *Ben Hur*. He oversaw the filming operation at the ranch but had time to visit between takes. The local cowboys admired him and his gift for telling stories about his movie and rodeo career.

A herd of buffalo, about thirty animals, was leased from a private herd in New Mexico and trucked to the Rocking R Ranch. The scenes called for a buffalo hunt, a stampede, and a shot depicting the trampling of a buffalo hunter played by a lifelike dummy. A big pit was dug for one of the cameras with a fallen tree trunk just above. When the buffalo were herded over the covered pit and log, it made for an exciting ground-level view of the oncoming stampede. The stunt double was filmed taking shelter behind the tree trunk to avoid being trampled. The buffalo charged as the stunt double took cover. A lifelike dummy was then substituted, and a concealed cable raised it to its knees directly in the path of the stampeding buffalo. A close-up shot made it appear as though the buffalo's hoofs trampled the hunter. When edited for the movie, the scene was very convincing.

In the next scene, another camera panned up the ridge where Chief Mad Dog, Buddy Heaton, looked on and took some pleasure in seeing the buffalo take a measure of revenge on the white hunter.

Several other scenes were filmed. One included a buffalo hunt, showing Indians firing arrows into the buffalo. Again, it all looked authentic in the final product. No one could tell the Indians were local cowboys in costume, World Champion Bull Rider Freckles Brown included. In fact, no actual arrows were fired from the bows of the would-be Indian actors. The arrows were added to the film at the Disney studios in California.

The whole thing was scheduled for three days of filming, but two mishaps slowed progress. The first problem could have caused injury to a camera operator. Most of the stampeding buffalo jumped the camera pit, though one buffalo tripped, fell, and rolled into the pit. The cameraman got the shot, jumped out of the camera pit, and ran for his life. The buffalo was not much the worse for wear, but when the movie was released, the animal's accidental few seconds in the camera frame made the final cut.

Yakima barked instructions, the grips moved the props, and the wranglers drove the buffalo over the camera pit repeatedly until the director yelled, "It's a wrap!"

Buddy Heaton, standing in for Iron Eyes Cody as Mad Dog, did a masterful job with one exception. The film was "in the can" in movie lingo until a technician and the continuity director reviewed the scene. They noticed Buddy had been wearing sunglasses during the final shot. Yakima was outraged and rued the whole scene would have to be filmed again because of Buddy's "damn fool mistake." The sun was too low to provide good light for the retake that day. A fourth day of filming was needed at no small expense for the production company.

Buddy Eaton's antics as a rodeo clown, actor, and cowboy were notable in Western movie circles, nevertheless, he was a professional, and this was seemingly an amateur mistake. He apologized to Yakima at length and then rode his horse to the corrals where the local cowboys were unsaddling their horses. Everyone felt bad about the costly mistake until Buddy said, "Men, these Hollywood boys got lots of money, and I figured these sunglasses would make us all another good day's pay. You guys don't owe me anything for my little screw-up, but I wouldn't mind if someone would unsaddle my horse and buy me a drink and a steak in Lawton tonight." I understand several of the local cowboys showed Buddy a rather fun time in town that night. It was also noted that Yakima and the film crew joined the party.

Yakima Canutt poses for a news photographer and reporter for a Lawton Constitution and Morning Press news release.

A news photo of the buffalo herd being filmed at the Rocking R Ranch for the Andy Burnett series was featured in an Associated Press news release. Reporter Bill Crawford was a staff writer for the Lawton Constitution.

This photo depicts an Indian actor in the process of firing an arrow into a running buffalo. There were no arrows actually fired, and the buffalo fell into a well-plowed patch of ground as the result of a trip wire. The buffalo was unharmed.

46. THE MEERS STORE

Meers Store was typical of most rural communities. You couldn't do much of anything that missed the attention of the regulars. Two people owned and inhabited the whole City of Meers which boasted only one city limit sign. Gladys and Lee Meyers were the store proprietors and presided over everyday activities. The locals dropped by to pick up their mail, grab a hamburger, swig a Virginia Dare, order a piece of homemade pie, and catch up on (or create) the gossip.

At one time, there was a much larger town with an economy based mostly on mining. It is estimated that as many as 5,000 miners dug for gold and other treasures in the Wichita Mountains. Meers was a hub with a population of a few hundred people owning or working at several businesses.

During the late '50s and early '60s, when we lived at the ranch, the store was the only structure remaining. The store offered a wide range of services including a gasoline pump, a US Post Office, groceries, a café; and some farm, hunting, and fishing supplies. It was mostly a forum for running conversations, gossip, and a friendly social life. With few tourists, the Meers store was a good place to hang out.

Lee was the target of many harmless pranks, and the more he let someone get under his skin, the more he clapped his false teeth. The habit was only slightly irritating, but it was considered a gauge of Lee's gullible nature and resulting agitation.

Dan Coates, Dad's friend from Texas, was clued in on Lee's temperament before his first visit to the store. Lee didn't know Dan from Adam when he walked in at noon one day with a briefcase and order form. About a dozen local cowboys were sitting at tables eating lunch when they overheard Lee inquire about what Dan wanted. Dan replied, "I'm taking orders for the power company on how many packages of electricity the store will need." Lee took the bait and swallowed the hook. The local lunch crowd understood immediately that Lee's leg was being pulled. They just kept eating and trying to stifle their laughter. Lee inquired, "What in the world is packaged electricity, and why do I need any?"

Dan had his story ready and explained the power lines were going to be rebuilt. Unless the store had a generator, his estimate of three packages of electricity per week would be enough to get by on. Lee said, "Well, I guess I haven't got a choice, but how much does this cost?" Dan explained, "The packages are free, as long as you promise to return the empty containers and agree to buy electricity from the power company after the lines are rebuilt." Lee inquired, "Where else could I buy it?" Dan said, "Mister Meyers, after you use this packaged stuff, you may like it better than the other kind, so we just want to be sure we'll have a customer later." Lee signed the ticket. Dan left the store and came to the ranch to spend a couple of days with my folks.

Everyone in the community, except Lee, soon knew about the prank, and for weeks Lee kept telling everyone they better sign up for packaged electricity. Later, when Lee discovered the scam, his teeth rattled at a record pace.

The Meers Store as it appeared in the 1950s.

A modern-day aerial photograph of the City of Meers with the Wichita Mountains in the background. Courtesy of GW Aerial, Elgin, Oklahoma.

251

47. ODDS AND ENDS

Dad loved unusual animals. While living at Meers, he found and purchased a giant, spotted trick mule named Big George. In the winter, Dad would bring Jimbo, his giant steer, to the ranch to relax and enjoy some time off from his exhibit at Cache. Oddly, Big George and Jimbo usually kept close company in the pasture. We wondered if they were attracted to each other because of their unusual size.

Like Jimbo, Big George was a rare sort of creature. Big George was nineteen hands tall (seventy-six inches at the withers) and had a white coat with grapefruit-sized brown spots all over his body. Each spot was circled by a dark ring, and his ears were as long as a man's arm from elbow to wrist. We didn't take him away from the ranch often, but we did take him to parades and other places to advertise the rodeos.

Big George also did a dozen or so tricks, plus he had a rather good "handle" as a riding mule.

After Jimbo died, Dad bought two big Holstein/Brahman cross steers that weighed about three thousand pounds each, named Pete and Punk. They weren't as big as Jimbo, but the pair were large enough to brag about and merit a twenty-five-cent admission fee for a look-see.

When Dad was the horseshow superintendent at The State Fair of Oklahoma, he hired Bill Hill to work for him. Bill was a self-titled traveling promoter. He traveled to keep out of trouble, and he promoted about anything to make a dollar. Dad rented display space across from the horse barn at the fairgrounds. He put up a tent and a painted front wall to "ballyhoo" an exhibit for Pete and Punk. Bill acted as the "barker" for the exhibit and did quite well, owing to his convincing manner. The first year Bill and Dad split a small profit, but the next year Bill had a better idea. He persuaded Dad to lease space for two tents and two ballyhoo fronts. He could hire another barker and put Pete in one exhibit and Punk in the other. The idea gained Dad's permanent respect for Bill's promotional abilities. Not only did people pay twenty-five cents to see one steer, but they also paid an additional twenty-five cents to see the other. Every few minutes Bill and the other barker would fake a dispute over which steer was the biggest. Some people would spend several quarters going back and forth between exhibits trying to satisfy themselves as to which steer deserved the title of biggest.

Pete and Punk.

Eventually Punk passed away. Pete was still a big attraction, but when Dad saw an advertisement in a Billboard Magazine listing the "World's Smallest Full-Grown Cow" for sale he got in touch with the owner and purchased the diminutive "Queenie." Thinking he had another showstopper, Dad planned to put Pete and Queenie on display at the Rocking R Ranch rodeo grounds at Cache. Rarely things did not go the way Dad planned. In this case, both Pete and Queenie soon passed away, probably from old age.

Pete and Queenie were almost in show business together.

48. FRANK RUSH PRODUCTIONS

Dad came up with a novel idea in 1958, soon after he got everything moved and operational at new Craterville Park, Cache, and Meers. He started a side business called Frank Rush Productions to keep his bookkeeping accounts straight.

He already owned a stagecoach and a beautiful pair of sorrel and white paint Belgium draft horses named Chief and Squaw. Something gave him the idea of building a Santa Claus sleigh big enough to haul 30 or more people and pulled by his paint Belgium team. After all, it didn't seem unreasonable in the horse country of southwest Oklahoma, that horses might pull Santa's sleigh rather than reindeer.

As he often did, Dad called his carpenter friend Jesse Robinson. Jesse had just taken a job running Larrance Tank Company in Lawton. Larrance Tank had the equipment to build about anything out of metal, so Jesse and Dad drew a rough sketch on scrap paper, and Jesse went to work.

They started with a frame of a cotton wagon. Jesse roll formed the front and rear curves and made decorative runners to hide the wagon wheels. He measured, cut, welded, and ground down the rough edges, creating a very functional sleigh ride.

Frank Rush Productions Santa's Sleigh #1.

The sleigh was attractive and colorfully painted, and families loved the "Free Rides Courtesy of the Local Merchants." The sleigh had changeable tongues, one for the draft horses and a different tongue so it could be hooked to a truck for transport. High-pressure truck tires allowed the sleigh to be pulled easily, even when fully loaded. The fabricated stairs on sled #1 allowed passengers to load and unload easily.

Soon Jesse was put to work on a second sled. One can notice from these pictures, that Dad had Jesse fabricate the loading steps for sled #2 on the right side so passengers could unload on the curb.

Santa's Sleigh #2.

Dad never sold tickets for rides, instead, he always contracted with the shopping centers to pay a flat fee thus making the rides around the center's parking lot free to the shoppers. Another rule was his wagons never operated on public streets unless the streets were closed for a parade.

Eventually, after our family moved to Arlington, Texas in 1966, Dad added two more sleighs, two stagecoaches, Santa's Trolley, and a dozen or so horse-drawn wagons of various descriptions to his Frank Rush Productions collection. For most of the years FRP was active, he owned 15 to 25 draft horses. For parades, we had as many as eleven horse-drawn commercial wagons in the Fort Worth Stock Show Parade for 52 consecutive years. We booked as many as 7 wagons for 28 years for each 24-day run of the State Fair of Texas Twilight Parade. There were scores of other individual bookings each year from 1965 through 2018.

A window card advertising Santa's Trolley for TG&Y stores.

The estimated statistics of Frank Rush Productions deserve brief recognition. Even though we didn't have all the equipment in operation for each of 59 years, by conservative estimate there could be as many as five million people who climbed aboard Dad's wagons at shopping centers. FRP commercially sponsored wagon entries appeared in hundreds of parades and the number of spectators who saw them pass in review would also be in the millions.

By the mid-1960s, Dad had developed a good relationship and made most of the bookings for his Santa's sleigh wagons with TG&Y stores, whose corporate headquarters was in Oklahoma City. From 1965 until 1978 the National Finals Rodeo was held in Oklahoma City. Coincidentally, our interest in rodeo and the fact that we worked the Santa sleds at TG&Y stores in and around OKC in early December each year matched up perfectly for a little family fun. Dad was among the first customers to purchase season tickets for the NFR.

Dad was well acquainted with Clem McSpadden who was an Oklahoma Senator, a well know rodeo announcer, and the general manager of the NFR. Dad sold Clem on the idea of using our stagecoach during each performance of the NFR, so the various corporate sponsors and celebrities could be introduced. Clem loved the idea and promptly hired Dad for the job. The stagecoach was a unique new idea at the NFR and was used during every performance until 1978 when the NFR was moved to Las Vegas.

Dad offered to take the stagecoach to Las Vegas when the NFR moved, but the PRCA got a better offer. Benny Binion, owner of the Horseshoe Casino in Las Vegas, had attended the NFR in Oklahoma City. Not only was he instrumental in getting the NFR moved to Las Vegas, but he also owned a stagecoach pulled by six matching black horses. Mister Binion volunteered his stagecoach for free, and since the casino name was on the coach, he got publicity and recognition.

The stagecoach tradition Dad started still takes place at each NFR performance in Las Vegas.

The Frank Rush Productions story illustrates Dad's drive to work in the entertainment industry. Frank Rush Productions was started while we lived at Meers although our family operated the business until we sold Sandy Lake Amusement Park in 2018. It was a lot of work to produce all those events, but it was also fulfilling to help create golden memories for people.

Tom Self driving the Frank Rush Productions stagecoach in the National Finals Rodeo at the State Fair Coliseum in Oklahoma City. World Champion Bull Rider Freckles Brown was riding shotgun and contestants for Miss Rodeo America greeted the audience.

Dad driving his Frank Rush Productions stagecoach "4-up" with Mom as a passenger.

49. COMANCHE COUNTY CSI

In 1959, Dad and Mom were busy running new Craterville Park, the rodeo, the curio store at Cache, and our ranch and home near Meers.

As we often did, after new Craterville Park closed on Sunday evenings and after the busy weekends, Dad, Mom, Suzy, her boyfriend and future husband Tom Self and I would drive the 60 miles from the park to Cache to drop off Tom at his house. Then we would continue 16 miles north passing through the Wichita Mountain Wildlife Refuge and on to the ranch. Dad and Mom always carried the "payroll" or income for the week with us. Usually, there was a shoe box containing the money under Mom's feet in the front seat. Though cautious, in hindsight, Mom and Dad were not as prudent as they could have been.

Around eleven o'clock one hot dry summer night. We dropped Tom off and continued up the highway toward Meers. Suzy and I were in the back seat sleeping and nothing unusual happened until we were about halfway home. Suddenly, a car pulled up on the rear bumper of my parents Cadillac and started flashing its lights and honking, all the while trying to pass us on the narrow two-lane winding road. It didn't take long for Dad to hit the gas and reach a speed that would make it difficult to pass, even if it had been daylight. Mom screamed and Dad told Suzy and me to hit the floor. The bumper-to-bumper chase continued for a few miles passing the Rush Lake sign, the Holy City exit, and the Ceder Planting Site at the foot of Mt. Sheridan. At the north gate of the refuge, the pavement stopped, and a notoriously dusty gravel road took its place. Once we crossed the buffalo cattle guard the dust boiled up behind that big old sedan. The trailing car and whoever was driving had to back off by at least a quarter of a mile so they could see. I peeked out of the rear car window and watched as the glow of their headlights almost disappeared in the dust.

The next half mile of the road was straight, but when we reached the Medicine Creek bridge the road again got crooked as a politician. We flew past Wayne Rowe's house and quickly skidded around the front steps of Meers store. Across the Jimmy Creek bridge and past the old Meers school house we sped. Dad was giving the Caddy a loose rein, but the chase was still on. Another mile north, a sharp left turn at the section line, and heading west one more mile we approached the entrance to our ranch.

Mom and Dad had a hurried discussion, argument, altercation, dispute and general falling out over what to do. If we turned in the ranch gate we were cornered. If we kept going there would be plenty of places to put the white boat-sized Fleetwood in the ditch. Dad saw the lights on at Rex Buchanan's house just past the ranch entrance and on the north side of the road. He slammed on the brakes, slid into the driveway, and pulled up in front of Rex's screened-in front porch.

The unknown devils were still coming on fast but didn't realize the dust had cleared until they were a couple of hundred feet past Rex's driveway. While they were backing up and turning up the drive, I peeked out again to see what was next on the program. Rex must have been watching TV in the front room as Dad yelled, "Rex, get your gun, come quick, I've got trouble." Rex walked out in the yard wearing only a pair of boxer shorts and holding what appeared to be a 12-gauge shotgun.

When the chase car pulled up, a man started to climb out of the passenger side door, but Dad was ready for him. Just as his feet hit the ground and he stood up, Dad hit his door, pinning him between the car and the car door. In the near darkness, Dad jammed the knuckle of his index finger under the guy's chin and said "That's a gun barrel son. You move and I'll blow your brains out."

Meanwhile, on the other side of the car, Rex rested the imposing steel barrel on the windowsill of the driver's door and spoke, "Don't make a mistake or this might go off." I also heard Dad and Rex use a few other words to emphasize the content of the warnings.

The guy Dad "had the drop on" said he was a Comanche County Deputy, and they were trying to stop us from speeding. He produced a badge, but when Dad demanded answers to a few more questions, things didn't seem to add up.

Dad took the man's badge and billfold and warned him to get back in the car with both hands in sight. He told Rex to keep them covered and then told them to leave and not come back, "or else." Since Rex appeared to be locked and loaded, they followed orders.

After they left, we were all shaking. Rex's wife came outside to see what the ruckus was all about. Rex brandished a four-foot piece of water pipe in the porch light and told Dad it was a good thing it was dark enough that those guys didn't recognize his fake scatter gun. Dad held up his bent index finger, pistol style, and muttered something under his breath. Discovering that neither of them were really armed, in the near darkness, I swear they both turned a shade or two whiter.

Dad called the sheriff and by early the next morning the law had the two imposters in jail with an extensive list of offences, including impersonating an officer of the law. The badge had been purchased in a pawn shop in Duncan. The two would-be robbers lived a few miles east of Lawton and both men had long wrap sheets, and both men spent several months in jail following the robbery attempt. They also admitted they thought "Frank Rush would be an easy target," and they didn't figure he would put up such a fight.

The county sheriff made Dad a Citizen Deputy a few days later, and the story went around the community that "you better toe the line up Meers way 'cause Frank Rush was ready for trouble."

50. ROUGH TIMES

Dad delighted in being a business owner, and he never backed down from the challenges. As a family, we worked hard and played hard. There was never a day we were bored owing to his drive and encouragement. As the years flew by from 1957 through 1966, Dad was in his prime, but as time passed his daily involvement became a heavier stone to roll.

By 1959, Dad finally realized the Corp of Engineers would never make good on their word about compensation for additional moving expenses of Craterville Park. By then, Dad had invested a lot of money and built a handful of businesses. He kept all his enterprises productive and profitable until about the middle of 1965.

New Craterville Park was busy but being more than an hour's drive from our home in Meers, he couldn't be nearly as "hands-on" as he needed to be. His employees at the park were loyal, trustworthy, and hardworking, but they fell short when it came to Dad's and Mom's management skills. Even though new Craterville Park was running smoothly, there was an unfortunate condition that began to damage the park's attendance. Migrant farm workers were plentiful in the area during the harvest season. Recalling that, in the 1960s, there was a great deal of ethnic discrimination. The South was in turmoil, but less overt issues were present with seasonal Hispanic laborers. While they attended the park in good numbers it ultimately had a negative effect on regular customers.

The operation at the Rocking R Ranch in Meers began to have its problems as well. Dad's philosophy about raising high-quality purebred Hereford cattle, Appaloosa horses, and American Quarter Horses was making positive gains until the market for each breed cycled and turned down. Especially in the registered Hereford cattle market, the years around 1965 were remembered as a crash industry wide.

There were circumstances Dad couldn't control, and Dad did admit he made some errors in judgment. It's possible, that if the government had paid him what was promised, he might have weathered the storm. At any rate, juggling three businesses in three locations began to be more than even he could manage.

Dad sold new Craterville Park in an effort to return to a positive cash flow. But it was just a matter of time until the same fate would befall the ranch at Meers, and the Indian Curio Store and rodeo operation at Cache.

Dad's close friend and personal attorney, Woolsey Godlove in Lawton, advised Dad to file bankruptcy to hold off creditors until he could liquidate his assets. It was a tremendously embarrassing move for Dad. The resulting dispersal was a little better than a breakeven proposition, but not much. Dad and I had a conversation about the subject years later, and I could tell from listening to him that he still felt he had disappointed Mom, the rest of our family, and a multitude of friends.

After Dad died in 2005, I visited with long-time family friends Jerry and Paul McClung at their home in Lawton. Paul was the editor of the Lawton Constitution newspaper during the "Land Grab" and was a close friend to Dad in good times and bad. Paul stated, "Some people were saying your dad got too big for his britches. Most people, who really mattered, were sorry to see Frank and his businesses go down. Frank Rush paid off all his debts, and anyone who knew him figured he wouldn't stay down for long."

51. GONE BUT NOT FOR GOOD

Dad emerged from bankruptcy with some horses, his Frank Rush Productions collection of wagons, and a family willing and able to help him battle back.

You might assume, for a book about the Rush family and our connection to southwest Oklahoma, Dad's story would conclude. Indeed not. Every enterprise on which Dad would embark for the rest of his life would be a variation on a theme he learned in the Wichita Mountains.

The reason for leaving Oklahoma and moving to Texas fell in our family's lap out of the clear blue sky in January of 1967. Angus Wynne Jr. owned Six Flags Over Texas since the park opened in 1961. Six Flags was booming under Wynne's stellar leadership. Mr. Wynne was looking for a major new western-style attraction for the Texas section of his theme park. Dad had a lifetime of experience enabling him to produce a first-class Wild West Show and by the Grace of God, Dad hit a home run.

Soon, Mr. Wynne and Dad shook hands and signed a lucrative and beneficial agreement for both parties. By lucrative and beneficial for both parties, I'll explain. Dad sure needed the money and a boost back up the ladder of success. Six Flags Over Texas needed a new headliner attraction to maintain its momentum as an emerging leader in the theme park industry. Dad hired five of the finest western-themed acts available comprised of about a dozen performers. He called Dixon and Gus Palmer, our Indian friends in Oklahoma, and asked them to put together a troop of skilled and colorful dancers. Our family and about a dozen of our horses made up the balance of the cast.

For the seasons of 1967 and 1968, the Six Flags Over Texas Wild West Show was by far the number one live show attraction of the park as proven by daily exit polling of park guests. By the end of the second season, when Mr. Wynne sold Six Flags to the Pennsylvania Railroad Corporation, Dad decided he wanted to move on. After nearly 700 forty-five-minute, action-packed performances, Dad had replenished his spirit, pride, and bank account. At 55 years of age, he was again hitting his stride.

Dad took his introduction to standing-room-only crowds at Six Flags Over Texas "wild west show style" nearly 700 times in 1967 and 1968.

The Six Flags over Texas Wild West Show cast.

In 1971, the Rush family transitioned back into a family-owned business at Sandy Lake Amusement Park near Dallas, Texas. As six equal owners, Dad, Mom, Tom, Suzy, Vickie, and I worked to provide a place where families could gather for fun and entertainment over the next 48 years. Sandy Lake Amusement Park's attendance far exceeded that of both Craterville Park locations. For nearly five decades, Sandy

Lake Amusement Park was one of the most successful privately owned amusement parks in the nation. The park boasted the largest filtered swimming pool in Texas. It was the site of FunFest, the largest and longest-running privately owned school music competition in the nation. Sandy Lake Park Catering served many, if not the majority of corporate picnics and family reunions in the Dallas/Fort Worth area. Families visited the park in droves and made "golden memories" of their own.

In addition to the second and third Rush family generations living on site, the fourth generation including Tom F Self, David Frank Rush, and Jodi Ann Rush were raised and worked at the park. David became the park's Operations Manager after graduating from Texas A&M with a degree in Park Management. The fifth generation includes T J Self, Whitney Rush, and Taylor Cuccurullo, and each lived and worked at the park as well.

The Sandy Lake Amusement Park entrance gate and the finest herd of Shetland riding ponies anywhere.

Driving the Sandy Lake Amusement Park stagecoach are Tom F Self, Jodi Ann Rush, and David Frank Rush.

For the final 34 years of Dad's life, he enjoyed doing what he loved. One of the many things that Dad was a master of, he knew how to draw a crowd and entertain families in an uplifting way. He did that until he ran out of time on January 5, 2005. Sandy Lake Amusement Park continued operations until the property was sold for development in 2018 after 48 successful seasons.

Dad and Granddad looking forward to a bright future. c. 1926.

Frank S. Rush c. 1932

E. Frank Rush c. 2000

Seated in Dad's office chair, wearing a replica of
Granddad's hat and keeping warm in Dad's buffalo robe.
I was thinking about the past.
I hope this book depicts what I remember.

Frank Rush III

www.ingramcontent.com/pod-product-compliance
Lightning Source LLC
Chambersburg PA
CBHW071737150426
43191CB00010B/1609